"*Camilla is brilliant and intuitive. Her safe and beautiful work allows you to take your journey of living deeper in your truth to new levels. It is always authentic, in tune and always wrapped in her loving intentions that allow you to feel courage, faith and power in new actions you take out into the world*"

Elizabeth Berkley Lauren

"*The lessons I've learned from Camilla have touched my life deeply, and I've been in awe as I've watched her transform from a glittering TV star to shining her light and spreading her message in the world in an altogether more meaningful way.* It's Not You, It's Me *will shift your perception. The only question you need to ask yourself is are you ready?*"

Alison Tay, Editor-in-Chief,
Grazia Middle East

"*Camilla is the real deal: someone who has overcome adversity and simply wants to share what she's learned so others might do the same.*"

Mail on Sunday

"*Camilla first seeks out to resolve the issues within, then and only then focus on the opposite side of the argument through empty, understanding and above all kindness*"

Chris Marques,
Creative director and DWTS Judge France

"*It has been a true gift to experience Camilla's kindness and wisdom over the past several years, and here, in this book, is that same transcendent gift that so many others now have the good fortune to discover.*"

Clint Kisker, Producer

IT'S NOT YOU,
IT'S ME

IT'S NOT YOU IT'S ME

CAMILLA SACRE DALLERUP

HOW TO HEAL YOUR RELATIONSHIP WITH YOURSELF AND OTHERS

WATKINS

Sharing Wisdom Since 1893

This edition first published in the UK and USA in 2019 by
Watkins, an imprint of Watkins Media Limited
Unit 11, Shepperton House
89–93 Shepperton Road
London
N1 3DF

enquiries@watkinspublishing.com

1 3 5 7 9 10 8 6 4 2

Designed and typeset by JCS Publishing Services Ltd

Printed and bound in the UK by TJ International Ltd

A CIP record for this book is available from the British Library

ISBN: 978-1-786782-72-4

www.watkinspublishing.com

CONTENTS

DISCLAIMER

ABOUT THE AUTHOR

Camilla Sacre-Dallerup is a bestselling author, Life and Transformational Coach, NLP Master Practitioner Coach, Certified Hypnotherapist and a popular meditation teacher at Unplug Meditation, LA. She is the founder of the successful life coaching business Zenme.tv, which is based in Los Angeles, and sees clients in person in LA, New Zealand and London, and worldwide, via the web. Camilla has helped many clients, including celebrities, deal with stress, confidence issues, addictions and trauma. She is also a motivational speaker and holds workshops in the UK, US and New Zealand, which include "Design your ideal partner", "Reinvent me" and "Forgive and set yourself free". This is Camilla's third book for Watkins. Her first book, *Strictly Inspirational*, was published in 2015. Her second book *Reinvent Me*, an 8-step program, was published in 2017 and has been translated and published in multiple languages.

Before reinventing her own life, Camilla spent over 25 years as a successful competitive athlete in the world of ballroom dancing. She was part of the original cast of *Strictly Come Dancing* (the UK's equivalent to *Dancing With the Stars*) and after winning the trophy in 2008 she left to focus on her wellness business.

Camilla is a coach who walks the walk and she is constantly setting herself new goals. Since 2018 she has been the head judge on *Dancing With the Stars* in

New Zealand. Throughout her years of competing and working in the media, one thing became very apparent to her – when the body and mind are in harmony, you are connected and can be the best version of yourself, enabling you to deal with everyday situations from a very comfortable place. Camilla is passionate about sharing what she has learnt, using the tools that have helped her and her clients, to help others to succeed.

Warning!

This book will
make you fall deeply in
love – with yourself!

FOREWORD

by Yung Pueblo

We live in a special time in human history. A few unprecedented developments in our collective psyche are coming together to shift the world as we know it. Essentially, people are looking for more than they were taught was available to them – more happiness, more inner peace, more fulfilment, more healing and more freedom. They are aware that there are serious limits to the happiness that material things can bring them and are connecting their happiness not with the things outside of them, but with the ongoings of their mind. Mental health has become a global discussion, with serious actions taking place, at a national and interpersonal level, to support the wellbeing of the mind.

The growing popularity of the conversation around mental health and what constitutes real happiness is opening the door even wider for Eastern introspective practices and Western therapies to be globally accepted, respected and utilized. Meditation is no longer strange or new, seeing a therapist is no longer taboo, taking time to cultivate and heal our minds is now becoming more common.

More than ever people are seeing that much of what we have personally felt in the past is still inside of us – an emotional history that very much impacts how we feel, think and act. Achieving self-love is a combination of finding a way to release the things that have been accumulated inside of us, breaking old patterns that do not serve us, building new habits that support our happiness and giving ourselves the rejuvenating rest that is so rare, yet necessary, for our success in this fast-paced modern era.

Once people notice that they can be happier and that they have much to uncover and release, the logical next step is to seek the tools they need to build a real inner peace. One of the benefits of living in a globalized world is that the best healing tools that different cultures have created and brought forward are now more widely accessible than ever. Since people are in very different places and since we all have our own unique emotional histories, we each need to go out and find the tools that work for us. A practice that is challenging but not overwhelming will certainly help us in our personal transformation.

In *It's Not You, It's Me*, Camilla uses tools that invite us into ourselves in an accessible yet effective way. What is special about this invaluable book is that it is a gateway into the inner world, something that can profoundly lift our self-awareness so that we can better understand ourselves and thus understand the people in our lives. Though we all have different mental content, the structure of the mind is essentially the same – understanding the similarities between the human experience helps us to improve the success of our relationships. When we work on knowing ourselves, there is a natural expansion in our compassion and our ability to explore multiple perspectives. When we become familiar with our own inner landscape, we can better manage the ups and downs of life and respond to our relationships with greater wisdom.

Society is created by the relationships amongst individuals. If we can improve our relationship with ourselves and those around us, it can only have a positive impact on the world at large. As people continue expanding their self-awareness and using tools that can help them let go of the old and build the new, this will undoubtedly have a positive impact on our world.

Yung Pueblo

INTRODUCTION

The title of this book couldn't be any other than *It's Not You, It's Me* – please let me explain why…

I've heard those five little words more times than I can remember – so many of my clients and friends have been on the receiving end of them, as have I, and some have said them too. They have become such clichéd words and their sincerity is often doubted. People assume they're only said when someone is trying to find an easy way out of a relationship, but let's just consider that there might be some truth in them…

When my friend told me that her partner had said, "It's not you, it's me" to end their relationship, I said to her "Maybe it really was about him." She looked at me as if to say "What? Are you serious?" And I was. When I see clients in my coaching and hypnosis practice, it often becomes clear that the problem *does* lie with them, and that it is only by looking inward that they are able to heal their current relationship or build stronger relationships in the future. The biggest bonus, which I've had the joy of witnessing so many times, is seeing how the hurt, disappointment and frustration of relationship difficulties gave my clients the opportunity to go on an inward journey that resulted in them having a better relationship with themselves – finding respect, acceptance and, most importantly, a self-love that they'd never known before. And that's exactly what we are going to explore here.

What if I told you a challenging relationship – be it with a partner, friend, relative, colleague, or with your job, your diet, your body – is a challenge sent your way for you to find your way home to YOU. YEP, crazy, right? But hear me out. If you feel pushed to the limit, not good enough, frustrated or angry, then I trust that you are ready to feel differently and rise up. "It's not you, it's me" is such a powerful statement because it acts as a reminder that if you want to change something in your outside world, you have to be willing to go on an inward journey too. We are going to take inspiration from the words rather than dismissing them, so that you can take control and get back in the driver's seat of your life. You will discover how challenging relationships give you the chance to heal and improve the most important relationship of all – the one with yourself!

"Relationships are assignments."

Marianne Williamson

Facing up to you

To get the most from this book, I want you to be honest with yourself throughout – to peel back the layers to your truest most authentic self. Only then can true spiritual healing take place. I know that you may feel challenged whilst reading this book and going on this inward journey (taking a long, hard look at yourself rather than blaming a person or situation in your life can be tough), but I want you to know that it is my goal to serve and to hold space for you through my words. You deserve to feel the kind of love I know is possible for all of us, the one that comes from deep within that no one can take away from you and which brings with it an inner peace that no one can disturb. Let me remind you, you were born to shine, and to feel whole and complete within. You may think that what is challenging you right now in life is happening *to you* but it is, as author and motivational speaker Tony Robbins would say, happening *for you*.

Finding yourself

When you have self-love, you'll be more able to be true to yourself. I remember having a deep conversation with my husband when we first met and he said, "In life, you are really only truly yourself when you are by yourself." At all other times you are playing the role of partner, brother, daughter, mother, boss. I agree with this, but I believe the more authentic, honest and open we are with ourselves, the more we have the courage to take our *true* selves into a relationship. To do so we have to be self-aware, accept ourselves as we are and definitely love ourselves enough – this will give us the courage to say, "This is me, take it or leave it." Although it may take a lot of work to get to that point of self-belief and self-love, it means that we can be our true selves and not need to keep up a façade that eventually will crack. This is extremely powerful in any relationship. What I have seen in my clients who have successful relationships, and experienced myself, is that they are with people with whom they can be most themselves and people who love and accept them for who they are.

"You can't heal what you never reveal."

Jay Z

Breaking the negative cycle

As you encounter the same negative experiences and feelings in relationships over and over, you may ask yourself, "How have I ended up here again?" It is common for people to find themselves repeatedly in the same situation, for example with a lover, a colleague or boss, or by constantly trying to stick to a diet to feel better about their body. If that's where you are at, then please let me help you join the dots so that you can become aware of, and then change, the pattern that is blocking your divine flow – so you can start aligning yourself with what you really want to manifest into your life instead.

You may resist looking inward, perhaps thinking, "It's not my fault that my boss is rude and arrogant," but in any negative relationship there is something for you to explore. I believe that in this example a lesson has been sent to you in the form and shape of your boss, and if you want to evolve it's your job to find out what unhealed part of you that person is reflecting back at you. If looking at relationships in this way is a new concept for you, please don't worry – it will all become clearer as we work through the book together.

Let me warn you, though, to become self-aware and self-accepting, and make changes takes commitment to yourself and to doing the exercises daily, but the benefits are incredible. When you take full responsibility for where you focus your energy, life gets interesting. And it all starts with HOW MUCH YOU LOVE YOURSELF. Because when we love ourselves, we tend to respect and validate ourselves too and lots of other positive stuff that I can't wait to introduce you to. Sharing these tools that can support you in unlocking your power within is beyond exciting to me.

The work starts here

The only way you will truly reap the benefits of this book is by committing to doing the exercises and by starting to observe *your* thoughts, behaviours and patterns in the relationship areas you want to improve as you work through the chapters. I will help you to realize fully the power of your thoughts and how by disconnecting the energetic charge towards someone or something, you take control of the things you can change and allow healing to be initiated.

I am going to share from my heart the wisdom and tools that have helped me, and my clients, to navigate through life like a seasoned skipper through rough waters. Everything I explore and teach in this book is based on the magical transformation I witness in my practice every single day. Clients who start out despairing at the state of their relationships and end up repairing them or, if not, parting or making changes from a place of clarity. They do all this by improving their relationship with themselves and how they perceive everything around them.

There may be some tools you want to disregard as perhaps too spiritual for you, and there may be some you will love forever. I want you to know I appreciate you either way and I know that you will take from this book exactly what is right for you. I have written it with the truest intention of putting what I see working every day in my practice, all in one place, for you to know that you are not alone and there are tools out there for you. No matter how enlightened we are, there is always room to grow some more – we are forever evolving and learning, and that's the beauty of human life.

How to get the best from this book

To help you find your way home to your most fabulous self, I've broken the journey down into what I believe to be four vital parts: Self-Awareness, Self-Acceptance, Self-Love and Self-Care. Most people will benefit from reading the book from start to finish as each exercise moves on from the next, gently guiding you through the different stages from acknowledging to solving and healing those issues that are affecting the relationships you want to work on. However, if you want to just dive in and read snippets or try out particular exercises which appeal to you, that's fine too. Some of the exercises may seem repetitive, but this is intentional – it will help you to narrow down exactly what you need to work on and for the changes to sink into your subconscious mind.

Where an exercise requires you to write down answers and reflect, you'll see a 📝 symbol. You can use a notepad, your phone or even scraps of paper, but by writing in a journal you can keep a record and track your progress. You may find it helpful to look back at some of your answers and reflections as you work your way through the exercises.

There are also meditations throughout the book, which you can do whenever you need them and which I hope will become an invaluable self-help tool in your day-to-day life. Look out for the links to the meditations online too.

1. **Self-awareness.** When we are self-aware, we are able to observe our own feelings, emotions and behaviours. Once we are tuned in, we will become aware of the patterns and behaviours we are repeating and what we would like to change and improve on. I always tell my clients that being aware of an issue is the first step to

healing it. The tricky part is when you are not aware. I like to think of becoming self-aware as waking up. Once you are wide awake to what is working in your life and what isn't, and who you are surrounding yourself with and what you truly want to surround yourself with, you will start to make better choices for yourself with a newfound awareness.

2. **Self-acceptance.** We can't change a situation we are in or something about ourselves until we acknowledge it and then accept it. When you accept a relationship is over, for example, or that you are in the wrong career, that is the moment you can start the healing journey and make positive changes. Or when you accept that a behaviour or habit is not really working in your favour, you can get to work on how to change it or improve it.

3. **Self-love.** Once you're fully self-aware and self-accepting, you can truly love yourself, warts and all! And believe me no one is perfect! The love you have or don't have for yourself will be reflected in the relationships around you. You will learn how to meet your own needs before you look for someone or something to meet them for you. I've watched so many of my clients fall in love with themselves and it's the best thing ever – truly life-changing – and I can't wait for you to experience it too!

4. **Self-care**. This is last but definitely not least. Taking the time to care for yourself says a lot about how much you actually value yourself and your self-worth. I'm going to share all of my favourite tools with you in my 7-Day Self-Care Plan, so that you can rise and shine and be your best awesome self.

"If you don't love yourself, it's impossible for you to love others. You can't give away what you don't have."

Joyce Meyer

Your toolbox

Look out for the 'Your toolbox' sections in each chapter. These are the exercises I mentioned on page 6, created to help you move closer to and fall in love with your true self.

Now let's look at some of the techniques used, and some of the inspiration behind them, in more detail so they provide a useful reference point for you as you do the exercises:

Reframing: This is such a great tool for retraining the mind so that you can feel, think or see something differently. It's a technique often used in therapy or coaching allowing the client to perceive the situation from a different perspective. Later on I will share the "how to" so you can become a master of reframing in your own life and know you have a mind tool up your sleeve you can rely on whenever you are trying to work out an issue.

NLP (Neuro-Linguistic Programming): NLP is a tool that helps you to better understand words that you use and how they support you or hinder you – you are basically learning the language of your own mind. NLP includes different types of communication techniques that can help you change a behaviour or thought. An NLP tool I use a lot, and which I'm going to show you, is "Perception is projection", which helps us look at relationships as our mirrors.

Meditation: Everyone can meditate and it really is one of the most effective self-help tools. Research is continually proving more of the amazing benefits of meditation, including that it helps to lower blood pressure, improve concentration and decrease stress and anxiety. I am passionate about teaching meditation and sharing my passion for it, both as a teacher and as a student, because I have felt the benefits in my own life and seen how it has helped to improve the lives of my clients.

I am going to share some of my favourite guided meditations with you, some of which I have recorded especially for this book for you to listen to for free – just head to www.zenme.tv/mindtools.

A common question I get asked by people starting out in meditation is, "How do I switch my thoughts off?" So let's just clarify something here – you can't switch off your thoughts, even when you meditate. You have about 60,000–80,000 thoughts a day, so when your mind feels busy and like it's racing at 100 miles an hour it's because it pretty much is! However, what we learn through meditation is that we can choose what we focus on and practise over and over again, bringing our focus back to one thing. That might be your breath, a mantra, an affirmation or even a colour. For example, while meditating you might think, "I forgot to do xyz today" or a specific relationship issue may be going around in your head on repeat. You might want to dive into each thought that appears, allowing worry to set in, and start speculating on the future or worrying about things that have happened in the past. Instead when each thought arrives, acknowledge it, but then instead of diving into it, bring your focus straight back to your breath or whatever is your chosen focus point. When the next thought comes, because it will, again bring your focus back to your breath and so it continues.

You will slowly start to become the observer of your thoughts and adopt a non-judgemental approach, just allowing the thoughts to pass by like clouds in the sky. This practice for the mind is very similar to working your muscles at the gym – the more you do it, the easier it will become. And the most wonderful thing is that the more you practise, the more you will be able to use this skill in everything you do, becoming more present in every moment and able to give each thing you do your full attention.

Meditation will also help you to become less reactive in situations where a considered response is more helpful – it allows you time to assess. So as you meditate, invite thoughts and noises around you to come and go and know that they are a reminder for you to bring your focus and awareness back to your breath. I want to make something very clear here, allow for your practice to be whatever it needs to be for you, even the days where the mind feels super busy and you are less relaxed, it's still working. Every time you redirect your thoughts in meditation back to you practising focusing on one thing, it will serve you long after your meditation is finished. Sometimes it's the most relaxing thing you have ever done and sometimes it's not – it is whatever it is and that's okay. As author and Buddhist teacher Pema Chödrön said, "We don't sit in meditation to become good meditators. We sit in meditation so that we'll be more awake in our lives."

Mindfulness: Like meditation, mindfulness teaches us to allow thoughts to arise and for us to observe what is present in the moment without judgement. Mindfulness, however, can be practised throughout the day not only when you decide to sit down and meditate. You can have a mindful cuppa, a mindful walk or even a mindful bath as you give that one thing your full attention. You are present in the moment, simply sensing what is there right now – not needing to change anything or worrying about the past or the future. There is such solace when practising mindfulness because you know you can be with and feel however you are feeling at the time, negative or positive, and honour what is there – give it space and allow anything that needs to clear through you to do so as you simply observe and stay present to what is happening in each moment. Thoughts, feelings, sounds – there is space for it all.

Visualize: I learnt to visualize as part of my sports training when I was 13 years old and this tool has followed me through life like a dear friend. Visualization is more of an active meditation in that you are intentionally imagining something. When thoughts come and go, you can still go back to your breath to bring your focus back to what you are visualizing. I truly believe that visualizing a goal, dream or relationship as successfully accomplished or healed helps you to achieve it in reality. When you go within and get still in both meditation and visualization you allow for your breath and thoughts to slow down a little and for a certain amount of space to appear between each thought. In this space, clarity, inspiration, intuition, peace and calm can appear. You allow yourself to connect with your true self and to feel connected to your deepest desires and as Bob Proctor, motivational speaker, bestselling author, and contributor to the world-renowned book *The Secret,* famously said, "Thoughts become things. If you see it in your mind, you will hold it in your hand."

Affirmations: An affirmation is basically a positive or negative statement we repeat over and over again. We create these statements for ourselves and as we repeat them they seep into our subconscious mind and become what we believe to be true, our reality if you like. Throughout the book we will explore the importance of making sure the affirmations you use are positive rather than negative and help you create some powerful ones for yourself. It's important when creating the affirmation to remember to make it in the first person ie "I", and present tense not future tense. For example, "I am strong", not "I'm going to be strong." "I am full of energy and focused." Writing these positive statements on your phone or mirror or in your diary, and repeating them in your mind or out loud to yourself in the mirror, can really help you to achieve your goals.

Personal stories: I have asked friends and clients to share their stories of how they healed challenging situations and relationships by healing nothing but themselves. I hope you'll be inspired by what you read.

My wish is for YOU to create a loving relationship with yourself, which I believe is the most beautiful kind of relationship. The kind we dream of, filled with deep love, understanding, forgiveness, compassion and respect. Imagine entering into any situation and relationship with that in your toolbox. I know, pretty awesome, right? It's possible and you deserve it as much as anyone else in this world. And just in case you doubted it, it is as possible for you as it is for anyone else. All you have to do is to be willing to invest in yourself by committing to doing the work within. Align yourself internally with what you want to attract externally. It's time. Are you ready to explore the possibility of falling madly in love with yourself? Let's begin.

"We're all just walking each other home."

Ram Dass

I

SELF-AWARENESS

You may have picked up this book in the hope of finding a quick fix for your relationship problems, but although that might sound appealing, I know it wouldn't really benefit you in the long term. Because to truly attract and sustain healthy and happy relationships, you need to look inward and become fully self-aware. And the exercises in this chapter are designed to do just that – they will help you become aware of your behaviour, and of any negative patterns and beliefs, and allow you to observe and redirect your focus to those areas of your life you would like to improve. All you need is to be committed and disciplined in doing the work, and soon your inner strengths and qualities will be revealed to you.

The words "Know thyself" are nothing new; in fact, they go way back to the philosopher Socrates. He believed that people were motivated by the desire for happiness, but that they could only make the right choices and achieve happiness by truly knowing themselves. Only when we do that will we create deeper, more meaningful and harmonious relationships in every area of our lives. When Robert Holden, author and psychologist and "Britain's foremost expert on happiness", said "Your relationship with yourself sets the tone for every relationship you have" he was spot on.

So it's time to dive deeper, beyond the issues that are present in this moment and gain clarity, knowledge and understanding so that you can soar in your relationships and find true contentment.

"True power is living the realization that you are your own healer, hero and leader."

Yung Pueblo

Change starts with you

As my coaching and hypnosis business grew, both online and in LA, it became more and more apparent to me that the relationship issues clients were dealing with had a common thread running through them. They all required my clients to accept that they could only change how *they* responded to things, their *own* behaviour – not the person or situation they had problems with – and decide for themselves which traits they needed to improve. They would tell me about their issue, for example about the person who was making them angry or sad, but the only thing we could do anything about *right then and there* was a) find out why this person triggered them in such an extreme way and b) work on making them feel stronger, more confident, and calmer so they were able to cope better when they had to face that person or a similar situation again. As we all know, if it's a boss, colleague or family member, it isn't always possible to just walk away. Neither is walking away always the solution – sometimes it's better to stay and learn from it and heal the wounds that have been

"Every situation that triggers you is an opportunity to get to know yourself better and to grow."

revealed to you through being in a particular relationship or situation.

So my aim was to help my clients to navigate through tricky situations with more ease. What I found to my surprise in the early days of my practice was that when you improve your relationship with yourself, you fully wake up to the fact that it's the most important relationship you will ever have. When that's a loving, kind and respectful one, guess what… you will react differently to situations, you will choose differently and you will attract different things into your life. And even when met with difficult or selfish people you will be equipped to handle them without it destroying you or even, with time, disturbing your inner peace. Extraordinary people like Nelson Mandela and Mahatma Gandhi demonstrated very well the art and importance of self-mastery and the power of forgiveness to create inner and outer peace. I can promise you that once you have fully connected within, you will be able to handle most things with grace and peace.

"It's like working any muscle in your body – each time you are confronted with a similar situation, you will be able to deal with it differently and feel stronger within each time."

What do you need to heal?

I don't believe in coincidences. I have seen way too much synchronicity in my life to believe anything but that whatever happens is meant to be. I truly believe there was a specific reason why you picked up this book, if not consciously, then subconsciously. You will get an opportunity to heal whatever frustration, hurt and disappointment was on your mind when you did so, through the work we are going to do in this chapter and beyond.

By looking inward and becoming more self-aware, you will find the areas of your life where there is room for healing, where perhaps it's time to return home to you. Maybe you have detoured, maybe you have put the feelings and needs of others above your own and handed over the control of how you feel to someone else. Or perhaps you have been caught up in materialistic things or turned to substances, such as drugs and alcohol, looking to those to fill a void within. Wherever you have been searching for that one thing to fulfil you, my aim through this book is for you to realize you had it within you all the time. To know you are already whole and complete, and that you are love!

Noticing negative behaviours and patterns

When we raise our self-awareness – I think of it as becoming awake – we are able to notice negative behaviours and patterns we repeat that we would like to improve on. We can bring them to our conscious mind. According to scientist Dr Bruce Lipton, your life is run by your subconscious mind 95 per cent of the time and what is in our subconscious has been there since the first six years of our lives, so it's akin to having a child run our lives 95 per cent of the time! That is exactly how it can feel at times, especially when we get triggered. As adults we realize that some of those old patterns created in our childhood are not aligned with how we want to think, behave and react now.

However, unless we consciously work with mind tools to change or improve some of those patterns, we will subconsciously continue to act and react in undesired negative ways. Dr Lipton explains: "The major problem is people are aware of the conscious beliefs and behaviours, but not of subconscious beliefs and behaviours." However, he says: "Once you have become aware of the fact that invisible programs from the subconscious mind are running your life, then you are responsible for it." The good news is that you can access your subconscious and create change via meditation, hypnosis and affirmations, as you will learn more about throughout this book.

Let's look at what those patterns lingering in the subconscious mind from childhood can look like. Perhaps your parents split up when you were a child, leaving one parent devastated; such an experience may have made you grow up overnight – perhaps you took on the role of caring for the parent you were living with to help them through this difficult time. Then, later in life, that role is familiar to you, so you feel you have to save and fix everyone in every relationship you're in, but deep down you are tired and would actually quite like to be saved and looked after yourself – the child within you is longing for that love you yearned for but didn't always receive in the way you needed it. Or perhaps your parents fought a lot and you took on the role of peacemaker or stayed out of the way for safety, which made you stay in your shell as an adult. Another example is if as a child you had a very controlling parent, perhaps you couldn't voice how you really felt and so your go-to was to get angry or frustrated. Later on in life when you detect this kind of controlling behaviour in someone else, you will subconsciously react in the same way, with anger or frustration or even by being controlling yourself. However, at this stage in your life, this probably doesn't feel good to you – something isn't aligned and you know deep down there is another, better, way to deal with it. You don't yet know how to react in your desired way in the heat of the moment because you are still being triggered by the old pattern in your subconscious. You may long to resolve the situation by calmly and assertively letting the person know that you won't be controlled in this way, or you may simply recognize the controlling behaviour and move on because you know that's not for you and you have already healed that within yourself.

Another common behaviour to be aware of is being judgemental and critical of others and of yourself. This time-consuming and energy-zapping behaviour happens subconsciously for many people and can adversely affect your relationships, including the one with yourself. If you were raised in a family where it was common to judge everybody, this will be the norm to you. Through coaching and hypnosis I've seen great healing for my clients once they became aware of their judgemental behaviour and how they had learnt this from their parents or people around them as a child. Allowing yourself to be kinder and compassionate to yourself, and less critical of others, is so freeing and something we will work on in the self-acceptance and self-love chapters. It is often said you are your own worst critic, but if you want people to stop judging you and find harmony within and in the relationships around you, start by letting go of needing to judge yourself for everything and swap it with a newfound awareness and curiosity. Chances are you will inspire the people you meet to do the same.

"When you judge another you do not define them, you define yourself."

Wayne Dyer

YOUR TOOLBOX: RELATIONSHIP INVENTORY

Which relationship would you like to heal right now? Which one is frustrating, draining and confusing you? Look at the checklist below and work out what resonates with you right now.

My relationship with
- Money
- My body
- My partner
- My business partner
- My colleague
- My father, mum, sister and so on
- My.....................

Okay, let's take a look at how we can kick-start the healing here and start peeling back the layers to find the root cause of what is actually coming to the surface to be healed. It's not the person or thing, such as your money, that you need to look at, but what it triggers in you as you'll discover in the next exercise, Thought Mapping.

YOUR TOOLBOX: THOUGHT MAPPING

If you have read any of my previous books, you will know by now that I love to reframe. Being able to reframe on the go in our minds daily is really helpful and I will talk more about that later on page 116, but for now let me share one of my favourite tools with you to help you map your thoughts and then reframe them.

Let's get to work. Are you excited to start connecting the dots?

1. Grab two pieces of paper. (For this exercise, it is better to use scrap pieces of paper, so you can discard one at the end of the exercise. You might, however, want to write up your reflections in your journal afterwards.)
2. Draw what looks like a sun. In the middle, write the relationship you want to heal – the one you wrote down in the relationship inventory exercise on page 21. So it might be the person's name – perhaps it's your partner – or it may be your body, your work, money. It's best to focus on one relationship at a time and then repeat the exercise if you need to. Then on lines coming out from your sun, write the emotions and feelings this relationship brings up for you. First write the negative feelings (see examples, below) – we will focus on the positives in a moment.

   Examples might be:
   • Anger
   • Frustration

- Upset
- Exhaustion
- Not good enough
- Unfair
- Broken
- Tired
- Not heard
- Misunderstood
- Controlling
- Negative
- Rude
- Less than
- Not important
- Sad
- Anxious

Or you might want to write whole sentences about how the situation is making you feel. Just write exactly what comes to mind.

3. Now consider…

Is this the first time you've felt this way? Try to see if you could swap what you wrote in the middle of the sun with another person or situation at an earlier time in your life.

Take a moment to reflect back over your life. Put on a relaxing song, consider the words you just wrote down and just let thoughts flow in and out of your mind. Simply observe here. Allow yourself to connect the dots without forcing it or rushing yourself.

If it's a love relationship, you might find that it actually represents a previous relationship that didn't feel good – one that made you feel unhappy, stuck, lonely, controlled, sad etc. It's common to realize that this pattern has been around for a while and that your current situation is once again highlighting an open wound within. Joining the dots and having this deeper understanding can help to dissolve the situation altogether and release the power it has had over you.

4. Now go ahead and take another piece of paper.

We are now going to reframe (see page 8). Draw another sun and write in the middle the same as for Step 1. However, this time create your dream situation – write how you would ideally like to feel in this situation using positive feelings and emotions. Examples might be:

- Happy
- Respected
- Content
- Heard
- Calm
- Trusting
- Loved etc

5. Ask yourself:

What would healing this relationship or relationships mean to you? How would healing this or these relationships affect your life in a positive way?

Taking back control

There's often an element of control in relationships – one partner might be more controlling than the other – but what I'm really talking about here is having given someone else the control to hurt, disappoint or frustrate us. This often happens when we believe that someone will fill some sort of void within us. That they will fill the part of us that feels lonely, lost and not loved enough. The danger, of course, is that we are handing over the control, literally giving someone else the remote control to our emotions. This is a huge responsibility to put on someone else – that they make you feel happy, worthy or loved – because that also means that they can take this feeling away from you at any point. Imagine the emotional freedom and the kind of relationships you will attract when you feel happy, worthy and loved with or without that relationship. Suddenly you are in charge of your own emotional remote control and can choose your own frequency and levels – now that's empowerment.

Many people hold onto relationships and jobs, even put up with unacceptable behaviours, for far longer than is necessary because they are scared of facing the reality of needing to fill a void the person would leave or having to create financial freedom for themselves. It may be that you are staying in a relationship with someone who you no longer love because you are scared you won't meet anyone else or in a working relationship that no longer fulfils you. However, what I often explain to clients is that by staying they could be prevented from meeting the greatest love of their life or finding a better job. They will never know what could have been and are likely to end up feeling alone or lost in the relationship or dissatisfied in the job anyway. This is the time you might want to weigh up whether the pain would be greater by staying or leaving. Ask yourself: If I stay in this relationship or keep interacting with this person, at what expense to my own health and wellbeing? Then, if it's a relationship or situation that you can't avoid, ask yourself: How can I make sure I protect and respect myself?

YOUR TOOLBOX: RELATIONSHIP CHECK-IN

Check in with yourself for a moment and ask if these statements are true for you in relationships:

- "I don't need to be with you, I choose to be with you."
- "I am whole and complete with our without you."
- "I don't need to be working here, I choose to work here."

Notice what comes up as you consider these statements. It might help to write down your feelings around these.

Finding my voice

The first time I found myself in a relationship that made me feel so bad I could hardly get up in the morning was in my first real job as an apprentice in an estate agents. The lady who owned the firm believed in ruling with fear; we feared that if we didn't do it her way we would be fired. I'd never been in a situation like this and I had to figure out what to do about it. When I thought about other times I had felt this way, I remembered being bullied at school and how I had not spoken out because I was worried about the consequences. What I was feeling now was just like the hurt and sadness I felt back then. I had connected the dots. This situation had come around again in my life so that I could heal that scar, giving me an opportunity to ACT in a new and different way.

I weighed up my options: I could stay and be miserable or be brave and walk away, even if that did mean being out of a job.

At that moment, something within me clicked into place and I chose to fully respect myself. I realized that I couldn't expect others to respect me if I was allowing someone to treat me this way. When the lesson became clear to me, I stood up and said straight to my boss's face, "I don't accept being spoken to in this way. I'm quitting."

Then, instead of sitting at home feeling sorry for myself, I called the nearby estate agents and asked if they were looking to take on an apprentice. I had three interviews within the week and three offers. Working for the one I chose turned out to be the most magical years in a fantastic environment. That situation taught me that lessons and chances to evolve are all around us and that when we truly respect ourselves, our values and our beliefs, we attract into our lives people who respect us. I believe that the universe rewards us when we have the courage to live our lives authentically, and it did so for me by giving me the opposite experience – working with fabulous people who treated me well. I don't even want to imagine the miserable time I'd have had if I had stayed in that job or how bad I would have felt, because, trust me, even after being there a short time I was starting to feel drained, unwell and moody, and that would only have got worse. I had a lot of phone calls *from my colleagues saying how I had expressed what many of them had dreamt of saying for years. Looking back, I can see that this experience was literally the power of reframing lifted off the paper and into real life.*

"No one can make you feel inferior without your consent."
Eleanor Roosevelt

Dana Michele's story

"When I first walked into Camilla's office, I was so annoyed and had a pit in my stomach because I truly believed my boss had it in for me. I worked in a highly competitive environment as an executive producer and I had to deal with a lot of egos and different heads of department every day. It was like being a juggler most of the time and deadlines were tight, so the last thing I needed was a boss that seemed to hate me. I was completely convinced he was not supportive of me and definitely didn't respect me.

When I began doing the reframing exercise (see page 22) with Camilla, I started to connect the dots. I discovered that the situation I was in at the moment was in fact highlighting a situation from way back, and making me feel exactly the same way. Once I realized this, we started working on what pattern I was replaying here and what I needed to learn from the situation. After a few sessions I wasn't as bothered anymore about the way my boss was treating me. I gave it less of my energy and attention, as I had decided not to take it personally and I knew I was doing a good job. I focused on what I was there to do, instead of on his behaviour towards me. To my surprise when I finished the project the boss I thought hated me, invited me out for lunch to say thank you for the amazing work I had done and even bought me a thank you present.

What I learnt from this situation is invaluable to me. This work relationship highlighted to me a deeper traumatic situation from my past that I had not fully dealt with, where I was not able to stand up for myself. It had made me fearful of uncomfortable situations, like this one, where I felt unsafe emotionally. If I had carried on believing that my boss had it in for me and had taken everything personally throughout, I would have made life and work for myself way more difficult than it needed to be. Instead I tapped into my self-worth and learnt to stand in my own power, believing in myself, my skill set and the value I was adding to the job."

"If you don't like something, change it. If you can't change it, change your attitude."

Maya Angelou

An opportunity to grow

I regard bestselling author Marianne Williamson as one of the best spiritual speakers in the world. When I was writing my first book *Strictly Inspirational* I had just moved to Los Angeles and I was thrilled to learn that Marianne was doing weekly talks at the Saban Theatre nearby (you can listen to her talks online – see page 170). At one talk she spoke about a person who she didn't really see eye to eye with. She said the last thing she wanted was to constantly run into that person, but it kept happening over and over again. When she thought deeply about why the universe kept bringing her together with this person, she realized that each time was a new opportunity for them to heal their relationship. One day she took that opportunity and the relationship was healed by finally having a conversation. What I took from this is something I have passed on to my clients many times since. I tell them to have that conversation they have been putting off, but to remember to come from a place of compassion, with a desire to heal the situation. They must be prepared to listen and to apologize for their part, because if they choose to have the conversation to prove they are right and the other person is wrong they are putting up barriers to healing instead.

When teaching the principles of *A Course in Miracles* Marianne says, "Relationships are assignments made in order to increase the maximum soul growth of both people… It is as though a giant machine somewhere sees where you are wounded, and then picks out the person and situation in all of the universe in combination with whom you would most likely be healed." Doesn't this challenge us all to look at every relationship in a different way?

Marianne continues: "The ego sees the assignment as someone who will give me what I think I need to compensate for the lack that exists in me. But the universe is invested in your soul growth, not in your imagined need. The universe knows you have no need other than to remember you already are and have everything." Choosing to believe these principles has helped me look at even the most challenging relationships with optimism and curiosity, knowing that they are aiding my growth on a soul level rather than just annoying me and making me feel bad.

Negative self-talk

I often refer to the brilliant, and in my opinion must-have book *The Four Agreements* by Don Miguel Ruiz; it's one I tell all my clients to read. I have learnt some invaluable life tools from it, which I use daily. Two of these things are "to be impeccable with your word" and "don't take anything personally". One of my coaching methods is based on Neuro-Linguistic Programming (NLP) (see page 8), which also teaches the importance and power of how we use our words and communicate and how this can either hinder or help us.

I help my clients to become aware of choosing words to help and support them rather than restrict and limit them. Self-talk is one of my favourite things to focus on with clients who are trying to heal a relationship. I really listen to the words they use to describe themselves, or their situation or issue, and then encourage them to do the same. An example might be making them aware of saying, "I'll never change that" instead of "I haven't changed that yet" – the first is a strong statement, a belief that something will definitely never change, whereas in the second statement the person is open to possibilities of what could happen. Another one might be a keen runner saying, "I'd never be able to run a marathon" instead of "I hope to run a marathon one day". Or "All my relationships are the same, they never work out", "The people I meet always end up letting me down" – these are both very strong statements with no room for hope. They could be swapped with, "I used to struggle with relationships", "I used to meet people who would let me down but now I choose differently". Saying "used to" helps frame it as something that happened in the past instead of something happening currently. The examples I have used here are likely to be said casually at first, and then they become the story you tell, and believe about, yourself. This then turns into a limited belief that restricts your possibilities in life, holding you back from what you desire. Negative self-talk can also be horrible things you say about yourself like, "I'm not enough", "No one loves me", "I don't like the way I look" and so on.

Later in the book I'll ask you to become even more aware of your self-talk and get you on a positive path by constantly reframing any negative self-talk into positive (see page 116). For now I would simply like you to become aware of how you speak about yourself and others and the words you find yourself using a lot about the relationship you want to heal. These words will be very revealing and help you eventually improve your self-talk.

So many everyday issues can be resolved with good, honest and clear communication, whether that's with others or yourself. Sometimes when I'm working with a couple it's magical to watch them solve their differences and issues right in front of me by simply being mindful of the words they use. Many problems occur because a person's ego gets in the way, preventing them from being open and honest, which leads to misunderstanding. Often we might not want to "lose face" – we might fear looking stupid or just need to be right or take the credit for something. When people seek relationship coaching or therapy, they are able to move into a space beyond the ego to find a more neutral common ground where the main aim is to resolve the issue. In this safe space, they can listen with compassion and actually understand where the other person is coming from. Even if they don't agree, they can usually come to a place of understanding or acceptance. I wrote a whole chapter on ego in my last book *Reinvent Me*. If you want to read more about whether your ego is getting in the way of your healing and stirring things up for you, check it out.

CHECK YOUR ENERGY

If you are tired or in a bad mood, become aware of how you are feeling before you decide to interact with any potential energy-zapping people or situations. You could protect yourself by, for example, making sure that you are prepared mentally, and that you have meditated and had enough sleep. The key is to not leave it up to chance. In the self-care chapter (see page 134), I will give you more tools to help you take care of your health and wellbeing. The stronger you are both mentally and physically, the better able you will be to deal with any person or situation. When we are tired or rundown is not the right time to address things because issues become magnified. It is better to rest and then look at everything with fresh eyes.

"Everything is vibration"

So believed Albert Einstein! Words, vibrations… "What?" I hear you ask. Not to get heavily into quantum physics here, but science has led us to believe that everything is energy and that everything is vibrating at different frequencies. You may have heard of the Law of Vibration and the Law of Attraction, that "like attracts like", meaning what we speak of and think of, we attract more of. I find all of this fascinating and it has inspired me to be mindful of what I'm vibrating or emitting into the world. There is a very apt quote: "You know the truth by the way it feels." When we are speaking or thinking angry words, it doesn't feel good within, your mood drops and you start to feel low and doubt yourself. On the other hand, if you think positive things about yourself, or even remember a time when everything felt good, you start to feel more upbeat and positive about yourself and the situation you are in.

So when you reframe a situation from a more positive outlook your vibration and what you are sending out into the universe changes. Think of a time when you chose to be nice to someone who was unpleasant to you, and you watched their mood and tone change to match yours – your vibration and suddenly the situation became less uncomfortable, perhaps even pleasant. Or think of a time when you doubted that something would happen, but then decided to simply believe and trust that all would be okay and suddenly everything turned out in your favour.

Esther and Jerry Hicks, authors of the #1 *New York Times* bestseller *Money and the Law of Attraction*, and many other fabulous books, are masters in the area of law of attraction and vibrations. Years ago when I was struggling to make it in my previous career, I knew I had to change my relationship with money to fully align myself with my dreams and desire of living a life of abundance. Going through a financial struggle personally brought up all the limited beliefs I had created around money, mostly inherited from what I had learnt or listened to growing up. Even if parents have the best intention at heart, how they speak about money and their actions can affect their child's beliefs about it. Examples might be that however much money there was it was never enough, or money instead of time or affection was given to show love. The child learns that love is conditional or that money is love, or if there is anxiety around money they might fear it will run out.

I wanted to change my outlook on money and switch it from one of lack to one of abundance, so I used to read Esther and Jerry's books and listen to their financial abundance meditation on repeat. Their work hugely inspired and supported my belief of the power of reframing and the power of our thoughts. The teachings include, "When your vibration shifts, your point of attraction shifts, and, by the powerful law of attraction, your manifestational evidence or indicator must switch, also. You cannot talk consistently of the things you do want to experience in your life without the universe delivering the essence of them to you."

This works for the negative thoughts we put out there, too. So becoming aware of how we talk about a relationship or an issue makes us aware of what we are actually asking the universe to bring more of. If you want abundance in your life, you have to start talking about money with great love and not lack. If you want a great relationship with your boss or with a lover, you need to become aware of how you are talking about the relationship you are currently having or not having because remember what you speak of you attract more of. So if you are constantly complaining about everything that is going wrong, guess what… more things will go wrong and the relationship you desire will be even further out of reach. Instead, start talking about what you do want and use all the enticing words to make the situation as healed and desirable as you want. Improving how you think, feel and speak about that relationship will help the situation change in a positive way and help you attract what you are ultimately looking for.

THE POWER OF WORDS

If you still need some convincing that the words we speak can affect us both positively and negatively, let's look at some more research. Firstly, an experiment by scientist Masaru Emoto in 1990 on energy and vibration, to find out the effect words have on energy. As our bodies consist mainly of water, he wanted to show how negative words can affect our health. Emoto explains that water that's free from impurities, when frozen, will form beautiful ice crystals and look like snowflakes under a microscope. Water that is polluted, however, will freeze without forming crystals. He found that the same would happen with water when he poured it into vials and labelled them with negative words. After 24 hours the water was frozen but not crystallized in pretty shapes – instead under the microscope the shape looked incomplete like impure water. On the other hand when he wrote positive words on the labels, like "peace", "thank you" and "love", the water produced perfect hexagonal crystals. You can see the results and shapes in the bestselling book *The Hidden Messages in Water* by Masaru Emoto.

Secondly, in May 2018, Ikea carried out an interesting experiment at a school in the United Arab Emirates for

Anti-Bullying Day to show kids how damaging negative comments can be. They gave two plants the same amount of water, light and nutrition but then asked students to feed comments to the plants via a recording device. One plant would be fed only bullying negative words and the other one only compliments. By the end of the experiment the plant that had only been given compliments was thriving, while the plant that had been bullied was droopy and wilted.

There is definitely something to consider here. Why would we choose to speak to ourselves in such a negative way when it has such adverse effects? Having read so much about similar scenarios has made me become super-vigilant of the thoughts I choose to think and the words I choose to speak. I urge all of my clients to be so too, if they want to align themselves with a vibration of joy, love and happiness.

YOUR TOOLBOX: WHAT NEGATIVE STORIES HAVE YOU CREATED?

Look at the questions overleaf. You might want to write the answers now or reflect on them for a couple of days. Notice what stories come to the surface. As you write them down, start to become open to rethinking and rewriting them if they are not serving you in the best way. Consider the relationship situation on your mind whilst observing your answers.

- What story are you telling others about yourself?
- What story are you telling yourself?
- What story are you telling others about your relationship situation or any other issues you may be facing?

Notice whether the story is positive or negative. Become aware of how the stories are aligned or not aligned with what you really want. Examples might be, "It always ends up like this for me", "It's not my fault", "I never seem to be able to communicate in the right way", "I'm useless at relationships", and so on. If your stories are positive already, carry on to the next exercise.

A great way to start is to become aware of words and phrases that have a negative vibe, which may be keeping you stuck or limiting your healing process, such as:

- Never
- Not possible
- Always like that
- Same thing every time
- I always end up in this situation
- Won't happen for me
- Maybe I don't deserve it
- I'll never have that
- I'm misunderstood
- Nothing I do is ever good enough

Start to introduce words into your story that are showing you there is hope and possibility of change, such as:

- I hope to
- I would like to
- I'm excited to try a different way
- I embrace change
- I believe people change
- I trust things will work out for me
- I have learnt a lot
- It wasn't personal

And then ultimately change the stories and incorporate positive-led words that show you completely believe that change or healing is happening, with statements such as:

- I believe it's possible
- Change is happening
- I am noticing I'm doing things differently
- I'm looking forward to what's next
- It's easy for me
- Things always work out for me

YOUR TOOLBOX: HELLO BEAUTIFUL!

This will give you a taster of mirror work to help prepare you for the mirror exercises later on in the book. I'm aware that doing this exercise may feel a little uncomfortable or even confrontational at first and that's okay. Approach it with an open heart and mind and be reassured that although it may feel silly at first, you will get used to it – just allow yourself to be playful.

Stand in front of the mirror and without judgement notice the words that flood through your mind as you stand there looking at yourself.

Please write them down in your journal.

Are the words kind? If so that's awesome.

Are the words not so kind? If so, that's okay too, that's why we are doing this, to help you become aware of what you are putting out there about yourself, so you can start to create a more kind and positive way of thinking and talking about yourself.

Think for a moment about how you talk about someone you love and appreciate? Imagine being able to speak about yourself like that straight into the mirror. For now we will leave it here having raised your awareness. We will revisit this later in the self-love chapter where we are going to do some serious loving on ourselves (see pages 122–4).

And, by the way, when I was a dancer I spent a lot of time standing in front of the mirror criticizing my moves, and my arms for being too long and lanky flouncing about in the wrong direction and not toned enough, and my legs for not being strong enough, and that I had no shape and that I was as flat-chested as an ironing board, so trust me, I know all about negative self-talk! Still, on a bad day, I'll point out a wrinkle I haven't seen before and think, "I'm getting old." Oh yes, we are all wired to think negative thoughts more easily than positive ones, but we can train ourselves (see page 116) to catch ourselves in the act and quickly reframe them in a way that supports us better.

A change of perspective

Taking inspiration from the NLP (see page 8) tool "Perception is projection" I will help you look at your situation from a different perspective. Really notice what you are projecting and what is reflected back at you. Through the exercises you will start to become more and more aware of what is in your control to change and how when making these changes within, it can improve the situation that was causing an issue.

YOUR TOOLBOX:
WHAT ARE YOU PROJECTING?

In the relationship inventory on page 21 you worked out the current relationship or situation you are working on. With that in mind, write down answers to the following questions:

What is the relationship or situation reflecting back at you and why is it bothering you?

Then ask yourself:

What am I projecting onto this relationship?

Examples could be it triggers anger, controlling behaviour or sadness. When you think about it more deeply, you may notice that you have been projecting frustration, jealousy or tiredness. It's important you use the words that are right for you here.

Don't judge the thoughts that arise. The first thought that pops into your mind is usually helpful, or you might need to think about it for a couple of days or sit with it in meditation (see page 9). Once you realize what the situation is highlighting to you, you will be able to start to consider what you can take responsibility for and the lessons you can learn, heal and evolve from.

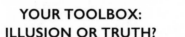

YOUR TOOLBOX: ILLUSION OR TRUTH?

We often build up a situation in our heads to be far worse than it is, going over it countless times, when we could simply stop it escalating out of hand by asking ourselves a few quick questions. Use your journal to write the answers and reflect on them.

1. Is it personal?
   It may feel like it's personal, but is it *really*?
   How will it serve me positively to believe it's not personal?

2. What are my thoughts about this situation?
   For example, your own behaviour, how you react, how you carry on or not.

3. What is my belief about this situation?
   For example, I don't agree with this person's behaviour and actions. It can be solved etc.

4. Is the other person acting from a place of malice or are they unaware of their own behaviour?
   This is important because ignorance is very different to malice, and being ignorant and unaware can be understood, even forgiven, if it is not necessarily aligned with your beliefs.

5. What is my belief about this relationship?
   For example, we have nothing in common, we
   misunderstand each other, there is mutual respect
   and so on.

Asking this last question, "What is my belief about
this relationship?" is a big one. Your answer will give a
lot away about the place you are acting and responding
from. Let's say your belief is "It won't last", "I don't
deserve him/her", "I'm not really qualified enough and I'm
going to be found out", "I don't like him/her".

These are all negative beliefs and the words have
a low vibration (see box, page 36). Indirectly you are
putting out negativity about that situation or person.
Even if it's subconsciously, it can be felt on an energetic
level by the other person. We will dive into the role
values and beliefs play in any relationship on page 49.

It's not personal!

By becoming self-aware, we better understand our
reaction to people and situations, and this can help us to
not take things so personally. One of my clients was upset
and frustrated by her boss, who would shout and blame
other people when things went wrong. I explained that
her boss was probably unaware of her behaviour and how
it impacted on people and that to behave that way she was
clearly in pain and turmoil within. My client felt singled
out, but I told her to consider that it wasn't personal. I

explained that her boss would probably behave and speak like that to anyone, which helped to ease her stress. Rather than trying to change her boss's behaviour – something that would be impossible to do unless she realized herself that she had an issue – her job was to figure out what it was triggering in her, in much the same way I had with my difficult estate agent boss (see pages 26–8). When you remove the emotional charge behind how you are feeling, you can start to deal with the situation in a more rational manner with less emotion. I realize, by the way, that arriving at a place where you can allow yourself to observe a situation for what it is and not take it personally takes work – a lot of work even – and you might even decide to not bother, but that will bring its own issues in the long term, like the behavioural pattern repeating itself in a different relationship.

The two ways my client could behave were worlds apart. Imagine how she would behave and feel if she took it personally compared to if she didn't. When you don't take a situation like that personally, unless of course it's actually bullying or worse, and you take it to the HR department, you will act from a place of calmness, strength and dignity and a response from this place will be more effective than one based on feeling hurt and having a bruised ego. If a pattern like this repeats in your life, however, it is time to look at why that is happening and work on what you can change within your behaviour – what learnings there are to help you move on. It's worth acknowledging, though, that these kinds of challenging relationships often are the greatest teachers. And, of course, once you have learnt from them you might move on or find that the person who challenged you moves on.

I see this all the time with my clients – things naturally evolve once we have learnt what we needed to from a person or situation.

Resisting change

Resistance can be a huge roadblock and stop you from truly blossoming, if you aren't aware of it. When I start working with a client, they always ask me how long I think it will take for them to change a pattern, behaviour or habit. I tell them that it depends on their willingness to make the changes, starting with taking responsibility for what is in their power to change and how much resistance there is, if any.

You have to work through resistance before you can tackle the actual issue, but how do you recognize that you have resistance? Well sometimes it can be a reluctant feeling, a worry or fear of what lies ahead of the changes, uncertainty of how to navigate through it. Sometimes you might be unaware of what is lingering in your subconscious, literally believing that everything that is happening is happening to you and not for you, being comfortable playing the victim and feeling sorry for yourself and blaming everyone else for your problems just so you don't have to do the work. Yes, sometimes others are to blame, but, remember, we cannot change other people's actions, only our own and, with practice, we can definitely control how we react to things. You can choose to feel sorry for yourself and let the things that happened define you or you can rise from the darkest of situations like many people who have gone before you. Nobody said, by the way, that making changes, evolving and becoming your best most awesome self was going to happen overnight or be a walk in the park but it's your life, your journey and wouldn't it be a shame not to know what loving yourself fully feels and looks like and what it means to blossom fully into your awesome self? I would say it would probably be the most important emotional investment you will ever make.

As we looked at on page 31, our self-talk can be very limiting. I often hear comments such as "I can't change", "That's just the way I am", "I was born like this", "I have always been like this". However, fascinating scientific research is providing more and more evidence about neuroplasticity – the brain's ability to adapt and change. The research proves that the brain *can* change and that it's not static as once believed. Every time we repeat an emotion or a thought we reinforce a neural pathway, which means that with every new thought we start to create a new way of being.

One thing I stress to my clients is the importance of having a disciplined mind; if they want to change something, that means repeating positive thoughts and affirmations again and again. The hard part is that as we are trying to make changes we find the brain wanting to go back to the old way because that's what it finds familiar. As Rick Hanson, Ph.D. and author of the wonderful book *Buddha's Brain*, explains, the brain is bad at learning from good experiences and good at learning from the bad. The brain has a negativity bias, which was what helped to keep our ancestors safe from threat in the past, but now it's more of a bug that blocks good and positive experiences. He also explains that we learn faster from pain than from pleasure and that negative interactions have more impact on relationships than positive ones.

So what we can take from this is that retraining your brain isn't quick or easy. You have to be tenacious when making changes and be aware that they won't happen overnight. But with perseverance, like anything you train to do, it becomes easier and eventually automatic the more you repeat it and rehearse it.

"A disciplined mind brings happiness."

Buddha

YOUR TOOLBOX: TACKLING YOUR RESISTANCE

Let's find out if you are resisting change. Answer the following leading questions in your journal:

- What am I resisting?
- Is making changes igniting fear within me?

If, yes, what do you fear will happen if you make these changes? Could you consider what is more fearful to you:

- Being stuck in the situation you are in and similar situations again and again?

Or
- Making changes and walking into the unknown? But with the possibility that awesome things could happen for you and everything could work out better.

If, for example, you are feeling lonely in a relationship, why stay for fear of being lonely without it? You are already feeling lonely or maybe worse anyway! You have everything to gain and really nothing to lose. In fact, taking that leap may give you the kick-start you need to go to work on your loneliness within and fill your own cup up with love until it overflows so much you will be happy with or without someone in your life.

"The people we are in relationships with are always a mirror, reflecting our own beliefs, and simultaneously we are mirrors, reflecting their beliefs."

Shakti Gawain

YOUR TOOLBOX: STAYING TRUE TO YOURSELF

When I see a relationship break down, or misunderstanding and miscommunication, it is often because the values and beliefs are not aligned between the parties. Self-awareness also means we know who we are as people and what we are willing to accept and invite more or less of into our lives.

Grab your journal and write down the answers to the following questions, it will help you know yourself a little better:

1. What are your personal values? (The things you believe are most important to the way you live, such as respect, honesty, loyalty, commitment).

   Make a list of your values.

   Being fully aware of your own values helps you communicate more easily what you are looking for from the other person and notice quickly when this is not a match.

2. What are your personal beliefs? (What you believe to be true about yourself in your relationship to yourself and to others.)

   Make a list of your beliefs about yourself in relationships.

   Make a list about your belief about that relationship.

   Examples of beliefs that can be damaging for you or your relationship:

   - Jealousy – all men/woman cheat or jealousy shows that he/she loves me
   - You can't have everything
   - The other person will change to suit you
   - That a relationship doesn't need work
   - I won't ever find anything like this again so I'll stay
   - I don't deserve to be happy
   - Nothing good ever happens to me
   - I'll never be happy

You may find that if the story you had created about yourself was not supportive, which we looked at earlier, there may be some limited beliefs here that you would want to reframe (see page 34).

Being aligned

When our values and beliefs don't match our behaviour, we feel off or like things aren't flowing for us. However, when we live in alignment with our values and beliefs, we feel good about ourselves and that things are fully synchronized. The same goes for any relationship; if we don't share the same core values and beliefs, it's difficult to really flow together and those relationships take more work, effort and energy. If, for example, one of your beliefs is that family is the most important thing and you are faced with someone who believes you should choose work above everything, or you want to have a child and your partner doesn't, you are never really going to agree on that part. The same goes for the workplace – you may be expected to work 24/7 when all you want to do is work part-time. And you will have to come to terms with what you are willing to compromise on and what you are not. When you are at home with your family and it's late and your boss calls you about work, do you ignore the call or take it? Start to really notice and become aware of how your actions make you feel when these issues arise, in the same way I asked you to become aware of your words. The feelings will reveal if you are living in alignment with your values and beliefs.

In the relationship you are working on – whether that's with your partner, a colleague, or a friend – what do you believe are your strengths, limitations and qualities? You can extend this to consider the other person's strengths and limitations, which will help you gain clarity on the relationship.

Manifesting what you want

Becoming self-aware and aligning yourself emotionally is vital to manifest successfully, which also means having the courage to walk away when you know deep down this is not your equal emotional match, or even a relationship you want to be involved in professionally or privately. As you've raised your self-awareness throughout this chapter, it has probably become more apparent to you what you really want to manifest into your life. However, if you let fears, including a fear of ending up alone guide you, I can pretty much guarantee you will not make the decisions that are aligned with your heart and soul.

What I live by and see every day in my practice with my clients is that you become a magnet when your actions are aligned with your heart's truths. Your manifesting strategy doesn't work when you feel one thing and do another. This is why so often people who are playing games at the beginning of a relationship end up completely miscommunicating and it ends up in tears. And when you want to manifest a great relationship, whether in love or your career, listen to your intuition. Sometimes we confuse our fear with the intuition so notice how your intuition is talking to you through your gut feeling and through your heart.

YOUR TOOLBOX: BECOME A MASTER AT MANIFESTING

To become a master at manifesting there are a few things to remember:

1. Align yourself emotionally with what you want to attract ie walk the walk.
2. Embrace an attitude of gratitude every time your thoughts drift into a lack mentality.
3. Know your worth.
4. Be present – practise through mindfulness or meditation.
5. Be open and aware of signs guiding you closer.
6. Be specific with your thoughts and words and be patient.
7. Tune into your intuition and listen.
8. Trust in yourself and the universe – your heart knows the way.

I have recorded a special manifesting meditation for you – just head to www.zenme.tv/mindtools to listen to it now.

Self-reflection

Spending time on self-reflection every day is a super-important self-awareness tool to help you better understand your emotions and learn about yourself and your strength and weaknesses. It doesn't matter how long you dedicate to it, even 5 minutes makes a difference. What matters is that you do it, especially if there are certain issues and relationships you have been trying to work out recently. At the end of each chapter, I will ask you to take some time to reflect on what each part of the book has stirred up and brought forward within you in the hope that it will inspire you to create a similar practice for yourself to continue after you finish the book. And of course know that you can revisit the book and its exercises like a trusted friend and go through it whenever you have a relationship issue that's bothering you, to gain clarity and deeper awareness of what that relationship is representing.

Self-reflection is not only a great way to honour our feelings, it's a great tool to use to make sure we don't just suppress them. As David R. Hawkins, M.D., Ph.D. explains in his book *Letting Go*, if we brush our feelings aside we still function but the pressure of burying those feelings can lead to irritability, mood swings, insomnia and many other conditions. He is not alone in writing about the effect that suppressed emotions can have on our health let alone our behaviour. Louise Hay and Deepak Chopra have shared their knowledge of this subject in their books and have hugely inspired me to listen to the messages my body is sending me. I'm passionate about the importance of the mind–body connection as I will talk about further in the self-love and self-care sections. As well as self-reflection, later on we will look at ways to become better at observing and accepting what arises using mindfulness tools.

YOUR TOOLBOX:
RAW-FORM JOURNALLING –
DOWNLOAD YOUR THOUGHTS

I've suggested you have your journal to hand as you do the exercises (see page 6) as it so powerful and helpful to write down your learnings, thoughts and ideas. I believe that something happens when we write things down – I call it downloading our thoughts. The process of journalling allows you to start to observe your actions and behaviours as you are writing them down, with a different perspective because you are not all-consumed by them. It's kind of like if you were swimming through murky water unable to really see anything, let alone the fish around you, but you might be able to feel them and then suddenly everything clears and you can observe the fish with awe and be inquisitive of the many different types.

So it is with your thoughts – suddenly by writing things down everything becomes much clearer. I carry a notebook with me most days, or use the notes app on my phone, and I often find that journalling flows best after I'm more relaxed, perhaps after meditating or going for a walk, or after having a hot bath or sitting down with a hot cuppa. It's important to write down whatever comes to mind without needing to judge or edit it, allowing it to flow in its raw form. Simply observe and be inquisitive of what you are writing – "That's interesting" or "I didn't know that bothered me as much as it clearly does" or "Why am I still obsessing over this?" and so on. This, combined with the other exercises you are doing, will gently help you move through the challenges. Some of my clients find it extremely helpful to journal in between sessions to heighten their awareness.

Mind Maintenance

To help you stay with this feeling of self-awareness, I'd like you to do the following every day for a week:

Meditate: Take a few minutes to connect to your breath by simply saying "calm" on the in-breath and "relaxing" on the out-breath.

Reflect: Start to reflect on the following sentence: I am ready to perceive this relationship differently and heal what is here to be healed within me.

Journal: Write down what came to mind, without judging it. Doing this exercise every day is interesting because you will slowly, over a few weeks, start to become more aware of your own behaviour and notice things you were unaware of doing.

> "Knowing others is wisdom, knowing yourself is Enlightenment."
>
> Lao Tzu

Now that you have raised your awareness, are you ready to dive deeper? Let's go. See you in Self-Acceptance.

2

SELF-ACCEPTANCE

So, great, you've worked through Chapter 1! It's truly my hope that you're feeling much more self-aware, which is a really powerful first step in coming home to yourself. I now want to look at accepting those things you've discovered, which can be a difficult but necessary process. Whether you need to accept something about a situation you're in or something about yourself, we're going to tackle it together here. Perhaps you've become aware of a life situation you need to change or improve on and it's time to face up to the position you're in, or maybe you've come to realize some of the repetitive negative behaviours that you need to address. Self-acceptance is such an important part of starting your healing journey to happiness and contentment. It's a chance to take that step in the right direction with a fresh perspective.

"Greater self-acceptance improves emotional wellbeing."
Srini Pillay M.D., author and Assistant Professor
of Psychiatry, Harvard Medical School

Time for change

The moment we accept that something has to change can be painful. My clients usually book in for a session when they are literally up against the wall emotionally with nowhere else to go and the pain is too much to handle. That's the moment they realize they are not super heroes, and neither do they need to be, and that something has to change if they are to feel better. You see, what's so interesting is that we really are all a bit like super heroes every day – we are so amazing at coping with whatever is thrown at us. We even get used to navigating through and handling certain difficult situations because we recognize the pattern and have perhaps been used to doing so from an early age, but let's remember that coping and actually living are two different things.

A few weeks ago, I went to another talk by the spiritual guru Marianne Williamson and she said something along the lines of "challenges and difficulty are never convenient – the wars were not convenient, illness and loss is never convenient" but now that the challenge has arrived we have to accept it and deal with it. We can't just look the other way. She's so right – the truth is we would all probably rather not have the rug pulled from beneath us and face going through a turbulent time, but accepting and embracing it, however painful that is, will help us get through it more easily and come out stronger on the other side, than if we resist it or pretend it's not happening.

Accepting a situation

It can be so hard to accept that, no matter the amount of pain, frustration or sadness something or someone has caused, it's out of our control to change it, especially if it's something from the past. Choosing to accept is much like choosing to forgive (see pages 90–1). It doesn't mean we agree with what has happened, but it means we accept what is and start from here. It means that we stop letting the past hurt our present.

Acceptance doesn't mean becoming resigned to the fact that "This is it and there is nothing I can do about it." It means saying to yourself, "Okay, this is where I'm at" or "This is who I am" and then asking yourself "Now what can I do with what I have? What are my options?" It can be the start of your journey towards all and more than you have ever dreamt of.

When we accept, we release the fear, anger, hurt and resistance that we have been carrying, which are all things that would otherwise act as a block to our personal development. You may have to accept that your relationship is over; that you've lost someone close to you; that you've had a disagreement with a friend; that you're in a career you are no longer enjoying or that's no longer for you. As we looked at earlier, often people wait for someone in their life to change – be it their partner or a difficult colleague – because it would suit their needs better. Accepting that the person isn't going to change and stopping trying to control them and their journey can be a huge step forward – and, more importantly, it frees you to focus on yourself instead. Similarly, in a work situation you may have to accept that this isn't the career for you, or the right company for you. Accepting that and moving on, rather than waiting for change, is so empowering.

Let's be real here. I know it can take some work to get to the point of acceptance. I remember clearly how it feels in moments of complete confusion when a friendship or business relationship is over, or the hurt and loss when someone suggests that you accept that, for example, a deep relationship is over, it's done, it's gone. WOW, those are probably the last words you want to hear in that moment and you feel more like telling the person to shut up than thanking them for their honesty and kind advice. It's like literally being dumped into a big great hole alone, screaming for help, only to realize no one is going to come and save you – you are going to have to do it yourself. In that moment of acceptance you have two choices: you can give up and give in and simply wait for that saviour who may never come and even if they did it would be like putting a band-aid on the scab, or you can become resourceful and figure out exactly how to save yourself. It will empower you hugely knowing that you are the one to save you.

People are amazing when they are pushed to the limit – that moment right there, that's when you become resourceful. The warrior, the goddess and the inner strength wants to come out, so you start looking at all the possibilities.

As many inspiring people have shown us, both in sports and business, what may seem like a hindrance or major setback can in fact become your biggest asset when fully accepted and then embraced. Look at Oprah Winfrey, a now powerful and inspiring philanthropist and media executive, who has led the way for so many people, showing us daily that the sky is the limit if you apply yourself. It's well-documented that Oprah suffered sexual abuse at a young age. Her life could have turned out very differently if she had become defined by that and let those wounds hold her back; instead she flew to the highest level possible in her life and daily inspires others with her learnings through her books, talks and foundation.

Amy Purdy, a Paralympic bronze medalist, motivational speaker and co-founder of Adaptive Action Sports, is someone else that has shown all of us how to reframe life on the next level. You might have watched her TED talk "Living Beyond Limits" – if not, it's worth a watch (see page 170). At age 19 she was diagnosed with bacterial meningitis. She was lucky to survive the illness but had to have both her legs amputated below the knee. Before losing her legs, exercise was always a big part of her life and she was determined to use her legs again and snowboard. So much had happened that was out of her control but instead of dwelling on what she had lost, she focused on what she had left, and strengthening her core muscles became her focus. Amy is such a perfect example of how to turn uniqueness into an asset. She went on to perform on *Dancing With the Stars US* and I don't think I was alone in sobbing the whole way through her stunning contemporary dance with Derek Hough. I have so much respect for her journey, her resilience and her grace. She often talks about how positive visualization was a big part of her recovery; she literally imagined what she wanted to be doing way before she was doing it. In an interview Amy explained that she decided not to "lie at home and feel sorry for herself but instead find a way to better herself in the world".

These are just a couple of inspirational stories that illustrate what is possible even when it seems impossible. It would have been so easy for Oprah and Amy to have become stuck in "Why me?" and focus on the pain, the hurt, and in feeling overwhelmed and not good enough, but they didn't –

"Challenges are an opportunity to up-level within."

instead they accepted what had happened and allowed it to fuel their journey forward, to push beyond limitations created by circumstances out of their control, and in doing so inspiring and giving hope to others.

These examples highlight the magic that lies in the way you perceive yourself and the power of making peace and accepting your situation and yourself fully.

Accepting yourself

It's one thing being self-aware, being aware of the habits and behaviours that have led you to where you are; it's another thing to accept those things about yourself. It's quite normal not to like or want to accept some of the things you've discovered, but it's only by accepting them as part of who you are that you can change them. You may have discovered things about yourself that you want to improve on – for example, wanting to have more self-belief, self-respect or confidence. You may have realized that by working on these traits, you'll no longer continue to make the same mistakes, such as choosing the wrong relationships or being challenged by particular kinds of people.

"This self-acceptance thing can happen in a moment of 'A-ha' or maybe more gradually as little by little you start to accept and embrace all that you really already are."

One important thing I'm going to show you is how to embrace what you've discovered about yourself and love your uniqueness. Self-acceptance is a chance to really recognize your own value, who your truest self is beyond the stories you have been telling yourself and others.

YOUR TOOLBOX:
ME RIGHT HERE, RIGHT NOW

Self-acceptance is about seeing yourself for where you are right now in this moment, not where you were or where you want to be.

It's time to tune in and gauge where you are on the scale of acceptance in this very moment. Go ahead and answer the questions below. You might sit and contemplate them for a while or write the answers down in your journal now.

This is how I feel right now in this moment of my life...

I accept..............about myself
I accept..............about the situation

Tune into how you felt as you completed these statements.

YOUR TOOLBOX:
MINDFULNESS EXERCISE

This mindfulness exercise, a Buddhist practice called Vedana, will help you to accept feelings rather than fight them – allowing them to be so that you can find peace with them – and stop them from spiralling.

Meditate for however long feels right for you, starting with 3–5 minutes (to time yourself, you can set an alarm or put on a relaxing tune if that works better for you). Relax and gently breathe in and out.

1. Allow thoughts to come up to the surface and acknowledge them without attaching yourself to them. Then label them in your mind with one of three words: pleasant, unpleasant or neutral.
2. Then bring your focus back to your breath. When another thought or feeling arises, observe it and label it in the same way as in step 1. Continue to do so throughout the meditation.

We like to label things in life, but by sticking to just those three words you will start to create pauses between your thoughts – some actual space. In that space you will find it easier to accept the things you have been resisting. It's such a relief to just know for that practice you don't have to be hard on yourself, judge your thoughts or get caught up in any negative self-talk – just allow whatever needs to come up for you to do so. Use only those three words so that you don't judge yourself harshly. Just accept all as it is in the moment.

Feeling overwhelmed

For most of us, finding our way home to ourselves and all the beauty that lies within is an ongoing journey and with some mind tools up your sleeve – not least the exercises in this book – I hope you will be able to navigate through the changes with relative ease. However, I'm very aware that it can feel overwhelming when we start to up-level ourselves emotionally as human beings, when we start to act and make decisions that are truly aligned with who we are at the core of our soul. The feelings that come up on our inward journey might be rather unpleasant and you may wonder "Will this feeling ever pass? When will I learn?" You may become impatient and frustrated, feeling "I'm doing all of these things but nothing is changing YET." It's at those moments that you perhaps even consider hitting the snooze button on self-development, but you understand too much already and know that if you bury your head in the sand now, the problems will still be there when you emerge.

I want to stress the importance of working with a professional whilst going through these challenging times and situations. If you are trying to accept something deeply traumatic that has happened to you in the past or are having to face up to and work on a difficult personality trait, a professional coach or therapist will provide a healing space and be able to advise and guide from a neutral objective place allowing you to find your answers in your own time. I remember the first time I reached out to a Life Coach – it was the best thing I did for myself at the time. It taught me so much about myself and really helped me evolve and heal relationship grievances, and it inspired me to become a coach myself. I was reluctant to seek help at the time because I felt like I was supposed to have it all figured out and just cope with whatever was thrown at me. I was worried I would look weak, but I know now that it actually takes courage, acceptance and vulnerability to admit you need help and that it's the best you can do to heal yourself. A therapist or coach won't judge you – he or she will support you in your healing journey. However, I would like to stress the importance of finding someone who you trust and feel comfortable with.

Turning to friends can of course be helpful – "a problem shared is a problem halved"– but sharing raw and unresolved issues with loved ones before you have even made sense of them yourself is risky. For example, you might not want to discuss feeling jealous, frustrated or worthless before working out where those feelings are coming from. Family and friends will care about you, and want to defend and protect you, so might give you a biased and unbalanced view. For example, if it's a relationship problem they might put all the blame on your partner and reassure you that you are not at fault for all the wrongdoings. Although that can feel good in the moment, in reality you are stopping yourself from actually figuring out what is going on and what this situation has come to teach you, even if the other person is in the wrong. Those close to you may also want to bring up a situation long after you have moved on, which carries the issue into the future when it should stay firmly in the past. If you have a friend or family member who can be objective then that's good, but it's not always the case.

Accepting responsibility

Whatever reasons there are for any relationship breakdown, even if one person has had an affair, there is always something we can learn that will help us grow as humans and there may be a part you need to take responsibility for. What I have learnt through years of working with couples is that there are usually many different parts to a relationship breakdown. Let's look at someone having an affair, for example: often both partners are aware that there are issues but denying them. Perhaps one person has repeatedly made it clear that they would like their partner to listen more, to be home more, to work less, to have more fun together, to make time for each other and so on – they have reached out. Maybe one person in the relationship, whether it's love, work or family related, was struggling in life and, instead of communicating that, numbing themselves with distractions such as other people, alcohol or drugs. In situations like this it's so helpful to accept what you can take responsibility for because when two people take responsibility for their shortcomings or mistakes a beautiful space is created between them. A space where accepting what needs attention can enable a relationship to heal or allow it to dissolve in a more amicable and peaceful way. When you put your ego aside and take responsibility for your part, you invite the other person to do the same and it becomes less of a blame game, which we know resolves nothing.

When one of my clients came to me heartbroken because she had found out her husband had been having an affair, we worked through her emotions and she eventually accepted that there was no way back for them. She felt so disrespected and hurt, but after a while she was willing to look at what she could take responsibility for in their relationship. She realized that her relationship with alcohol had become out of control and admitted that on many occasions her husband had let her know how much it upset him when she drank – he would say he felt shut out and that she didn't care about him. The sad irony was that she had felt lonely and neglected in their relationship, but hadn't communicated how she felt – subconsciously she had begun to fill the void of feeling lonely by drinking and it had become a daily habit and a cycle she struggled to break. She enrolled in AA, alongside coaching and hypnosis with me, and made great progress. In this situation, accepting that she had an issue with alcohol was a huge step towards her healing, but unfortunately in this case it had taken an affair and a break-up for her to truly admit and accept there were issues that needed dealing with within. Of course if I was dealing with the husband too, we would have worked out his underlying issues for having the affair. Her realization took the therapy to a whole new place and instead of working on her broken heart from her marriage ending, we started working on the root cause of her issues and on healing the void within her. It transpired that this stemmed from the lack of love she had felt as a child when she was constantly left alone, feeling scared and not loved. Of course it would have been better if she and her husband could have communicated clearly and listened to each other and worked together to heal their issues. I'm by no means saying that having an affair is the answer, but just that sometimes it's through the painful and hurtful situations that we learn our biggest lessons. It doesn't have to be like that of course, but it often is. If it doesn't hurt this much, then we aren't forced to look at what the situation has brought up. If the challenges we are sent are not too uncomfortable, we often don't learn the lesson – we just carry on as we are until the next challenge. As humans we unfortunately learn faster from pain than from pleasure, as we talked about in Chapter 1. Once my client worked on filling this void within her and on self-love, the next relationship she attracted was completely different. She was in a much better place emotionally and she has now come a long way from feeling lonely and empty to living a life where she feels fulfilled and loved.

Taking responsibility for our part goes for friendships and work relationships too. I remember a friend of mine highlighting to me, a long time ago, that she was always the one travelling to see me – she was totally right; I had just never thought of it this way. But I came to realize that what I felt, but had not communicated to her, was that although I cared for her I didn't feel we wanted the same from our friendship anymore; that our values and beliefs were different at this stage of our lives compared to when we were younger. My action had spoken louder than my words and I took responsibility and apologized for my part and we amicably took a step back from our friendship. We still loved each other from afar, and still do, but chose not to carry on disappointing and expecting different things from each other that we couldn't or didn't want to live up to.

YOUR TOOLBOX: FILLING THE VOID

It's so liberating to discover that you can fill a void yourself – you don't need to rely on something outside of yourself to fulfil you and make you happy.

It's extremely telling and healing to ask yourself:

"Is there a void within me I'm trying to fill?" and "What am I trying to fill that void with?"

Some examples might be:

- Food
- Sex
- This relationship
- Alcohol
- Drugs

What is the void? What feelings come up for you? Explore this by writing in your journal if you need to.

Examples might be feeling bored, alone, not enough. Answering this will help you to accept what the real wound is that you need to work on and heal.

Accepting I had to move on

I guess one of the most challenging times for me was when I found myself heartbroken in my 30s. I went from having landed my dream job on one of the biggest shows on British TV, buying my first home and being engaged to a great guy. Yay to me, I thought. The next minute I was walking away from all of it with my heart in my hands. Just like anyone else would when going through a break-up with a long-term partner, not long after you've gotten engaged, I went through the different stages of being angry, hurt, not quite wanting to believe or accept it and wishing everything would just go back to the way it was. I felt, of course, that would be easier than having to go through the awful experience of accepting it was over and the pain that brought with it. It was almost tempting to turn a blind eye and pretend all was still well. I even tried that but the pain of my broken heart was screaming too loudly for me to ignore it.

The acceptance did not happen overnight, I can assure you, and there were different stages of it. As my partner and I also ran a business together I had to accept that was over as well. Everything we had worked for was over. I kept wishing there was some quick way to get over this and when someone told me it might take me three years to heal I was in complete denial; it was just too much to think I would have to feel all of these nauseating feelings for that long. I tried blaming the other person at first but then realized that I had to accept the breakdown, understand the part I had played in us ending up in this mess and decide what I truly wanted to happen moving forward. Did I want us to resolve it? Did I want us to go our separate ways? And once I was clear on that I accepted both what had happened and my decision to go our separate ways. My focus then became healing myself, which included owning my part of the relationship breaking down.

"Whilst staring back at what could have been, you can't see all that can be. Turn around and look at all of the opportunities that lie ahead."

Looking back, this painful experience was one of the most healing experiences of my life and a big part of why I help so many couples in my practice today work through their differences and difficulties. I would like to think this whole experience has made me a more well-rounded and understanding person, coach and wife to my wonderful husband today.

Grieving

Accepting that we have to let go of something – a relationship, or a specific dream and goal – is difficult, and grieving for that loss is an important part of self-acceptance.

Tracey Cleantis, writer, speaker and psychotherapist, describes very well the art of grieving our unrealized dreams in her book *The Next Happy*. She makes very clear the freedom that follows once we close the door or, as she says, "let our dream die" in order to move on. The process of grieving our unrealized dreams is the same as when we grieve the death of a loved one – the way we experience it is individual to everyone and you can't put a time scale on it. If you have worked really hard towards something, invested everything, whether emotionally or financially, and then realized it's never going to happen it's important to recognize and accept these feelings that are coming up around that – you will be able to reframe them once you have worked through them and are ready. It is important to accept the uncomfortable feelings and emotions and explore them with curiosity rather than pushing them away. As Carl Jung said "What you resist not only persists, but will grow in size."

I have seen many clients frustrated and being so hard on themselves because a situation or relationship has not worked out the way they had envisaged; it hasn't lived up to their needs or expectations. Often the frustration and sadness is tied to what they think they "should" be doing by a specific time in their lives or what they think a situation "should" look like, comparing themselves to their peers. It could be that they are grieving a break-up or the dream of being married before they reach a certain age, or grieving the fact that their parents weren't there for them or didn't show love for them growing up – the fact that their family situation looked different to others they had seen. What we don't want is to hold onto the grief or somehow allow it to block ourselves from moving forward when we are ready. If we don't release these emotions and instead conceal them, they come out in all sort of ways, showing up in the way we react to others, mood swings or even health issues.

There are many ways our dreams and relationships can materialize and sometimes it's not exactly how we think it will look – but the new version of that dream can at times be more beautiful. One of my clients desperately wanted to have a child of her own. After doing round after round of IVF she felt depleted and upset and for a long time she didn't want to accept that it might never happen. She had to accept her situation and grieve her dream of what she had longed for. She had never considered adoption and was not open to it, but once she accepted the situation fully she started to look at having a child on a more spiritual level, from a place of believing that the child she was supposed to love and raise could still happen if she adopted or had a surrogate. She accepted that she had to let go of the dream of becoming pregnant and giving birth to her own child and look forward to the prospect of creating a safe and loving home for an adopted child to blossom in, knowing that she would be creating a beautiful relationship with that child. For others in a similar situation, it might have been accepting not being able to have children and focusing on a career where they could be of service to children, that would give them an outlet for that maternal love and a sense of purpose, although in a different way.

My clients sometimes want to focus on the time they have wasted in a relationship or in the "wrong" career, but

I truly believe that nothing is ever wasted – we can always take away valuable lessons. The amount of time they spent in that relationship may have been the exact time they needed to truly learn lessons and gain valuable experience. When we feel hurt so deeply that it's almost unbearable, it guides us to do some soul-searching and cracks us open – through the pain there is an opportunity to heal deep wounds that have been brought to the surface and which would otherwise lie dormant under the surface.

Letting go of my dream

When I left Strictly Come Dancing *(known worldwide as* Dancing With the Stars*) in 2008 as a champion my dream was to carry on as a judge on the show, something I had wanted to do rather than be on the dance floor since the very first season. After doing six years on the show, I didn't have it in me any longer to dance; my body was ready to retire, but I still enjoyed making TV and especially being part of such a special show, so it was with sadness in my heart when I finally announced I was leaving. When a position became available on the judging panel a while later and my agent put me forward, I was interviewed but the job went to someone else. I was livid and sad and it took me quite some time to accept that this simply wasn't on the cards for me at that time in my life. Knowing what I know now I can see how not getting that job at the time actually helped me to make really important decisions in my life that I might not have made otherwise. That included a move to LA with my husband, starting over in a new country, becoming an author and running a coaching business I once only dreamt of. If I'd have become a judge I would have perhaps stayed in the UK, made different choices and the five-*

year magical adventure I have been on in the US may have never happened. That is difficult to imagine now, given what an amazing learning curve it has been, both personally and professionally, building my business and connecting to so many amazing people all around the world, being part of their journey; it makes my heart overflow with joy every day.

I allowed myself to grieve that dream. I worked through the frustration, disappointment and rejection to accept it and to make peace with it and then refocus my attention on other areas of my life I felt passionate about. It took time and I did go through all the emotions and thoughts just like anyone else who has had to let go of a dream. However, as I completely detached from it, the universe brought it to me in a different way. In 2018 I was asked to be the Head Judge on Dancing With the Stars in New Zealand and I loved every minute of it, plus I approached the role from such a different place than I would have done back then, with a newfound awareness. So what I'm saying here is, although I had let it go, what's meant for us will flow to us.

> *"Every time I thought I was being rejected from something good, I was actually being re-directed to something better."*
>
> Steve Maraboli

YOUR TOOLBOX: GRIEVING AN UNREALIZED DREAM

This exercise is designed to allow you to grieve and accept an unrealized dream. Any suppressed sadness or frustration may come out as irritation when you are speaking to certain people or watching other people living out your dream. Use this exercise to make sure there isn't any sadness or other emotion lingering.

Take a moment to consider the questions and then write down the answers:

- I'm sad that..................
- I'm grieving that....................never happened
- I feel.......................that it turned out this way
- It makes me feel..............having achieved that

Voicing it helps you make peace with it and focus on all the stuff that has and can happen instead. Notice what the last word you wrote was. If it was, for example, "not enough", "sad", "angry", "hurt", you may want to spend some time healing that wound through meditation (see page 9) or mindfulness practice (see page 11). And consider what you are learning through allowing yourself to grieve this.

- What am I learning through this grieving process?
- What has happened or can happen as a result of my dream not coming to fruition?

If you're struggling to let go, take a look at the denial section opposite.

Denial

Sometimes when we are grieving something we so desperately wanted, there may be a certain amount of resistance to letting it go, or you may even be in complete denial, telling yourself it can still happen. Try to be completely honest with yourself here and ask yourself if there is still some resistance around the acceptance of the situation?

I have seen this many times with my clients in their relationship break-ups. The other person has clearly moved on, but they are not ready to accept it yet. They might say things like, "They'll come around", "They still love me", "We have so much history". Or sometimes it might be a friendship that has run its course, but you still carry on just to be nice, which isn't doing either of you any favours. Whenever we stay in a relationship that has actually run its course, whether friendships or love, we are actually not only blocking the opportunity for someone new to make their way into our life, but also blocking that space for someone new to come into the other person's life. Ask yourself what you are denying that's happening here and what you don't want to acknowledge, see or hear?

A mistake, not a failure

Accepting mistakes and your shortcomings is important, but that does not make you a failure. Remember you can still be a good person just because you are not hitting the targets at work or because you messed up in some way. Every human is a work in progress and we are all constantly learning.

In my 20s I rushed into relationships and in my 30s when I was eager to change careers I rushed into a new business idea and invested a handsome amount of money into it, although the idea of the business was interesting, I actually had no passion for it so needless to say it didn't end how I imagined. I pulled out of the deal and lost my money. I don't consider it a mistake because I learnt some valuable lessons from this – do your research, make sure you are passionate about it and get to know the strengths and weaknesses of the people you are going into business with. It's pointless having a working relationship with people who are all good at the same things; it's the differences that will complement the partnership. It's the exact things that may annoy you about someone that could be the one trait you are missing. If you are not particularly organized, for example, but your colleague is, that's great; or if you are more laidback and your partner is more driven, you may support each other – your partner will help you get things done, while you might help them to relax.

I remember sitting in a meditation class a long time ago when the teacher suggested that when we catch ourselves being harsh on ourselves, talking about our shortcomings we should say, "I love myself anyway"! I tell you what, if you try that for a whole week you are going to feel a whole new level of self-acceptance.

Gratitude and being able to forgive ourselves are also super important in the process of self-acceptance.

Self-esteem

Self-esteem is what you believe about yourself – and having high self-esteem means having confidence in your own abilities, and valuing and respecting yourself. I think when we accept ourselves for who we truly are, even the things we at first consider as our shortcomings, we can start to focus on our abilities. I remember, whenever I felt defeated as a child, my mum would always say "Believe in yourself and trust yourself, honey. Stop comparing yourself to others and focus on your own journey." These are words I have repeated to myself in many challenging moments. When we are focusing on all the things we don't like about ourselves, we aren't allowing ourselves to see all the beauty and qualities we do have to share with the world. And often the one thing we think is holding us back is something that actually adds to the dimension of who we are.

YOUR TOOLBOX: U-TURN YOUR THOUGHTS WITH GRATITUDE

Accepting what we have to be grateful for is such a useful tool. When I first heard Tony Robbins talk about using gratitude to switch your mood and thoughts from negative to positive I thought, "Really, it's that easy?" But I also thought, why don't I just try it in case it really works. I did and I have been using gratitude to u-turn my thoughts for many years now. However simple it is, I can tell you it really works. So when you get yourself all caught up in negative thinking about relationships, get going with the gratitude.

It's not just Tony who thinks this. Rhonda Byrne, bestselling author of *The Secret,* says "Gratitude is the fastest way to change every single thing in your life." And now it's also backed by science – research at UC Berkley found that gratitude has lasting effects on the brain. People who had practised gratitude showed greater neural sensitivity in the medial prefrontal cortex, an area of the brain associated with learning and decision-making.

So next time you catch yourself being negative, start listing in your mind or writing down things that you are grateful for to switch your focus from an unsupportive mindset to a supportive one. It can be as simple as being grateful for waking up today, for your body, for good health, for your hot shower in the morning, for a nice gesture from someone. It doesn't have to be materialistic, although you might also be grateful for the food you eat and the clothes you wear, or the fact that you have bought yourself a car.

Try to really tune in to the feelings around what you're writing. You can write a gratitude letter if you prefer. Do whatever works best for you. I spend a couple of minutes each morning in the shower giving thanks.

Let's go!

What are you grateful for?

....

....

....

....

....

....

....

....

Accepting myself

For as long as I can remember, I've always felt everything so deeply and I always felt it was a weakness. I would walk into a room and know if someone was feeling sad or uncomfortable. It was very overwhelming at times, especially when I was young. When I was in my 20s I never understood why being at busy events or in noisy restaurants would wear me out so much. Even spending a day with friends would be exhausting. In my early 30s I realized and accepted that I am "an empath" and a highly sensitive soul (yes, it's a thing and not just like wow you are sensitive, but more like wow you really do feel everything kind of way!). This used to really bother me because I just wanted to hang out with friends and not worry that I needed my rest – I felt I was boring at times. If I was out for an evening, the next day would be pretty much written off and that was without having a drink. I can't function without 8 hours' sleep and I need a lot of alone time to rest and reset each day, and socializing, flat-sharing or going off on girlie weekends would be challenging for me, especially before I learnt to accept how I was and how to create a life around it that worked for me. In the work I do today, I have come to realize that it is a gift to have empathy for others and being able to be so in tune with my feelings and intuition is serving me well as a coach.

YOUR TOOLBOX:
ACCEPT AND SWITCH IT

Now it's your turn. In this exercise I want you to answer the questions and accept the thing you believe to be your shortcoming and spin it on its head so it becomes a quality.

- I accept that I'm................................
- I think it's a good quality because it actually makes me............

Or

- I can learn from being.........and use it to.........

Some examples: maybe you are very quiet, especially in groups, and have so far thought it has held you back, but now you realize that it makes you a great observer and you make great decisions because of it.

One of my clients told me that he assessed people quickly, kind of judged them, and he didn't really like that. But he has realized that he is just a very good judge of character and that it has served him well and protected him at times, so he uses this skill of connecting with his intuition now in business and has learnt to trust it fully.

Self-worth

Accepting the way certain people are in our life can be very freeing. Sometimes it is those closest to us who will make us feel low and worthless, but it's important to remember that they can't make you feel that way unless you allow it. If they are going out of their way to make you feel that way, they have their own issues to deal with. If you can, you might want to break up with that relationship or friendship.

The moment you truly realize and accept that the other person won't change can be tough. I have been there many times with my clients and in my own life. You want so badly for them to realize that there is a different way. Healing yourself and leading by example is usually what serves best. Sometimes the person will notice your changes, come around and feel inspired, but this is not always the case. People only change when they are ready to do so, so it will depend if the timing is aligned. My client Catherine had a difficult relationship with her mother and had to accept that her mother would perhaps never change…

Catherine's story

"I came to Camilla for guidance because I had just come out of a controlling relationship. I was feeling lonely and struggling to communicate with my mum. All I ever wanted was for her to understand where I was coming from, to actually truly see me and hear me and for her to take responsibility for her actions and behaviours. Although I had had a fairly loving childhood, it often felt conditional – my mum was quite controlling, selfish and she loved to judge everyone and everything. She was completely unaware of her behaviour and how it affected the people around her, especially me, and if I ever brought it up she would get mad and never admit or even consider that she was in the wrong. Our relationship was tiring.

As much as I disliked her behaviour, at the age of 35 I found myself in a relationship that was starting to feel very much like the one I had with my mum – my partner was controlling and a narcissist. One day I woke up and thought "NO MORE", something has to change. I simply couldn't take this kind of behaviour any longer. I felt emotionally beaten down. That was the moment I walked out of the relationship and started my soul-searching journey.

Through Camilla's coaching and the tools she gave me, I became more and more aware of how in control I was of my own emotions and behaviour and how I could choose how much I let my mum's or anyone else's behaviour affect me. I started to accept that I could not change my mum nor did I want to (well maybe a little at first), and instead I focused on how I reacted and communicated in relationships like this. It made situations that used to be super uncomfortable more comfortable for me. What this healing time taught me was that a person can't change an issue they are unaware of. You have to accept that no one is going to change unless they are ready to do so and you cannot change anyone and neither is it your job to do so. Even if you try to make them aware, unless they are willing and ready to see it or hear it, there is nothing you can do but accept them as they are and then of course it's up to you whether you want to keep the relationship.

As I became more mindful and calmer, I started to approach conversations with my mum differently. At times she still makes me feel slightly frustrated, but ultimately I know that she cannot really disturb my inner peace unless I allow her to, and that makes it so much easier to communicate. Setting some much-needed boundaries in our relationship really supported me too. The acceptance also really helped me in managing my expectations, because I have realized that she can only give love the way she knows it and not the way I need it or would like it. I have let go of that expectation and therefore don't feel disappointed – instead I appreciate what she does give in her way. Our relationship is so much more comfortable now and I'm not sure if it's because I'm less reactive too, but she seems calmer and I feel in moments she even sees me for who I am."

What is interesting to acknowledge in Catherine's case is something I see a lot when working with my clients – we are attracted to what is familiar even if it doesn't really match our values and beliefs any longer. In positive psychology this is called the familiarity principle. What it means in Catherine's story is that because her mum was controlling and a narcissist, this was familiar to her and she was attracted to a similar situation in her love relationship. The same goes for relationships where someone has grown up with an alcoholic parent or a parent who is abusive; they sometimes end up in similar relationships as adults and it's often when they, like Catherine, find themselves challenged to breaking point that they seek help and start to realize the wounds or patterns from their childhood that have come forward to be healed so that they can choose differently in the future – choose in a way that is more aligned with what their soul truly yearns for, even if it's unfamiliar.

As you learn to respect and value yourself more, certain relationships you may have struggled with will become easier to deal with because you simply won't feel as triggered and you will be able to stay in your power and let them stay in theirs.

*"An unhealed person can find offence in pretty much
anything someone does. A healed person understands that
the actions of others have absolutely nothing to do with
them. Each day you get to decide which one you will be."*

Unknown

Let it go!

So once you've accepted that you need to look to yourself
rather than the person or situation that is causing you
difficulty, what tools are available to you? First let's look at
the habit we all have of letting things fester and then I'll
show you two really effective exercises – the Letting Go
Meditation and the Cutting the Cord Visualization.

"Love me or hate me, both are in my favour. If you love
me, I'll always be in your heart. If you hate me, I'll always
be in your mind." This quote by Shakespeare is so poignant.
It really describes perfectly how the things we give attention
to fester in our minds. I'm a huge believer that energy
follows thought or as James Redfield – author of, in my
opinion, the life-changing book *The Celestine Prophecy* –
would say, "Where attention goes, energy flows: Where
intention goes, energy flows."

When we are frustrated or angry with something or
someone, it's easy to go over the issue and keep replaying
it in our minds and discuss it with everyone we come into
contact with – this means you spend even *more* of your
precious energy on it. What happens in situations like
this is that you are actually the one carrying yesterday into
today. Even if someone was in the wrong and hurt you,
in this moment you are the one carrying it forwards and
hurting yourself by stewing on it. After endless reading over

the years, I have come to believe these negative thoughts are like poison to the body. They ignite the body's fight or flight mode and cortisol, which is the biggest stress hormone. Bestselling author Dr Lissa Rankin believes that by "changing your thoughts you can change your health". Imagine the effect on our health of re-running a negative situation over and over again. You will cause unnecessary harm to your body.

Once we have accepted a situation for what it is, what has happened and our own mistakes or shortcomings, we are ready to reframe and let go of any negative feelings and emotions that may be lingering. I have recorded a special meditation for you (see overleaf) to visualize letting go of whatever has come forward so far that is blocking you in moving forward.

Cutting off energetically as described in the visualization (see pages 89–90) means that even if you still have to spend time with someone or stay in a particular situation, it will no longer drain you of energy. You are now in control and choosing to reframe in a more positive way to suit you. I remember the first time the Life Coach I was working with introduced me to this cord-cutting visualization – it was after a break-up and I felt an immense relief. Now I use it whenever I want to bring my energy back to me and it has helped me become even more aware of relationships and situations that drain me.

YOUR TOOLBOX:
LETTING GO MEDITATION

The guided meditation is ready for you at
www.zenme.tv/mindtools.

1. Get comfortable and get ready to go on a guided journey.
2. Tune into your breath and let yourself relax a little deeper with each out-breath.
3. Imagine you are floating on a wooden raft down a gently flowing river.
4. Become aware of how the scenery is changing around you as you float, maybe the colors, the people, nature.
5. First imagine the situation, feelings and emotions you are letting go of surrounding you – maybe even notice how that feels.
6. Then imagine as you choose to let them go – float away and leave them in the past. You might just leave them where they were as you float away or imagine them being cleansed in the water beneath you. The surroundings start to change and perhaps you are now feeling lighter from having let them go.
7. Now you are surrounded by your ideal situation – how you would like to feel each day when you wake up, how you imagine yourself in situations and relationships where everything is flowing for you.
8. Allow yourself to float along the river for as long as you need to explore the different surroundings, enjoying this visual reframe and come back and open your eyes when you are ready.

YOUR TOOLBOX:
CUTTING THE CORD VISUALIZATION

Sometimes people really affect us energetically – it's that feeling when you just can't get them out of your head. Some believe it may be to do with a connection on a soul level, being soulmates, or a connection from a previous life. Whichever it is, it's a connection that runs deeper than usual and can really shake us up energetically. However deeply your energy has been affected, you can use this exercise at any time you feel drained by someone and want to bring your focus back to you.

1. Sit somewhere where you won't get disturbed where you can just relax, perhaps putting on a relaxing tune.
2. Close your eyes.
3. Spend a few minutes just observing your breath and allowing your body to relax.
4. Then bring to mind an image or feeling of the person you are having a relationship issue with.
5. Imagine that person standing in front of you and that there is an energetic cord between you. Notice where in the body it's connected to you and to them.
6. Then imagine your hand doing a karate chop or literally do it with your hand in front of your body.
7. Imagine the cord is cut now and the end nearest you flows back to you and goes within to close that gap and the other parts flow back to the other person, both returning to your own energy, regaining your inner power.

8. Even if it has been a difficult relationship to cut, send them away with gratitude for any lessons you have learnt through this relationship and love and blessings for them to find happiness and peace within. As we all know, that really is what we wish for all human beings to have, in spite of what has happened.

Enjoy the guided version of this meditation I've created for you at www.zenme.tv/mindtools.

I have heard a lot of magical things from clients after doing this exercise. Some tell me that they stopped thinking about that person or became less bothered by them. Some found it easier to forgive after cutting the energetic cord, and felt more at peace when that person communicated with them or saw them. Knowing that everything is energy, I believe that the person feels you having pulled away energetically and that you are slipping away and therefore reaches out, even though you aren't doing it for that reason. It's fascinating. If the connection is really strong, you may want to repeat this exercise a few times – as many times as you need to until you feel the energetic pull or emotions towards that person lessen.

Forgiveness

Forgiving someone doesn't mean you agree with their actions. It means that you are deciding to accept what is and honour how you are feeling, but that you are choosing to draw a line under it. You are not letting someone off the hook – you are forgiving to set yourself free and so that the resentment and anger can no longer hurt you. Remember you are carrying those negative feelings within you and the other person may have moved on long ago, so at this stage it's only hurting you and you deserve better. When you don't forgive, you allow yourself to carry the past into the present and pollute your life over and over again, instead of leaving it where it happened, in the past. This, of course, takes time and only you know if you are ready to leave it behind and choose you.

This is also true for forgiving yourself. It's extraordinary how hard we are on ourselves and how liberating it feels when we forgive ourselves. Sometimes it's as simple as forgiving yourself for a decision you made, something you said or maybe time spent in a relationship you knew deep down was not right. It's time. Let it go and forgive yourself, liberate yourself. You can use the letter of forgiveness exercises below.

"If you are withholding love as a form of punishment, who is being punished?"

Donald L. Hicks

YOUR TOOLBOX:
I FORGIVE MYSELF AS I FORGIVE YOU

I'll never forget the first meditation class I sat in when the teacher said, "Consider if there is anything you need to forgive yourself for." Lots of things flooded into my mind – I had been so busy forgiving others, I had completely neglected forgiving myself. I think most of us would immediately remember times where we have been hard on ourselves or felt bad about hurting someone else, or felt bad about a failed relationship, or bad about something we may have said in the heat of the moment.

Grab your journal and write a letter of acceptance and forgiveness to yourself for having been hard on yourself. Then write a letter of forgiveness to the person you are having trouble with.

It doesn't matter how short or long the letters are and you don't need to send or show them to anyone. They are just for you to clear the issue from your mind and gain a new perspective.

The letter can start as simply as

Dear [your name]
I accept that .... and I forgive myself for ....
The reason why I choose to forgive myself is because.............
I accept this because it makes me feel ....

Or

Dear [other person's name]
I choose to forgive you for ....
Forgiving you is allowing me to move on and ....

Carry on in your own words.

"Whenever you're confronted with an opponent, conquer him with love."

Mahatma Gandhi

Accepting without judging or comparing

Unfortunately there seems to be a comparison epidemic going on in society and it's causing a lot of stress and anxiety. People have always compared themselves to their peers – what they are wearing, who they hang out with, their achievements, how much they earn – but somehow social media has exacerbated this comparison. After scrolling through social media, most people are left feeling overwhelmed and "less than", hugely judging themselves for all the things that are not happening in their life. If you notice yourself starting to feel low and falling into the comparison trap of "I wish that was me", "I wish I had that kind of relationship, that job, money, body", STOP immediately and put the phone down or turn off the computer. Make a promise to yourself right now that you will not do this to yourself. This is not being accepting of yourself; this is self-sabotaging behaviour.

If you know it doesn't feel good to you but you keep doing it, try saying a positive statement to yourself when you feel your mood shift into a downward spiral, such as: "Thank you for showing me what is possible", or an affirmation such as "I accept myself as I am and I embrace my uniqueness. I have so much to share with the world." Comparing yourself with someone else does not serve you, so unless it fuels and inspires you to get on with your life and you see it as a way of being reminded if they can have

YOUR TOOLBOX: LET'S CELEBRATE YOU

A wonderful tool for self-acceptance is to allow yourself to celebrate what makes you YOU! Your uniqueness. I would love for you to list below all that comes to mind when you read the following…

My uniqueness includes being…….

It could be things like creative, funny, loyal, honest, a great listener, a great dancer. Now ask yourself:

If my best friend were to describe me, what would I like her to say?…………………………………….

Practising self-acceptance includes recognizing what you have already accomplished. List below the first 5 things that come to mind that you are proud of yourself for having accomplished:

1.
2.
3.
4.
5.

Some examples might be moving away from home and supporting myself, giving birth, getting a job, being there for my friend when she needed me.

that so can you, then stop looking at it! This goes for checking in with your ex on social media too. If it isn't fuelling your joy, then stop it!

"Others cannot see our full worth until we honour it fully ourselves."

YOUR TOOLBOX: MIRROR EXERCISE

Let's carry on from the mirror exercise in Chapter 1. If doing this exercise still feels too uncomfortable at the moment, don't worry. We are going to do more mirror work in the self-love chapter (see pages 122–4) so you can skip it and come back to it. However, I encourage you to try it. What's the worst that can happen? You will feel the same. What's the best that can happen? You will start to feel empowered and awesome. Just saying! Are you going to give it a go?

Can you look in the mirror and truly accept who you are, and embrace everything that makes you you? Have a look.

If yes, boom, well done, this rocks.

If not, what resistance are you feeling? What are you not willing to accept and why?

Consider:

- How is not accepting it going to serve you?
- How is accepting it going to serve you?
- What needs to happen if anything for you to accept it?
- Could you choose to accept it now?

Louise Hay is someone who inspired me and my work hugely. If you have never read any of her books, I urge you to do so. She was one inspiring woman when it came to positive affirmations and self-talk. I was aware of the principles and effects of negative self-talk, but hearing Louise Hay speak of the power of affirmations helped me take it to the next level and I will be forever grateful for her work. I will always remember the first time I read the affirmation by her "I love and accept myself fully" – it was so powerful. I look forward to helping you become a master of positive affirmations by the end of this book as we get creative with the affirmations in the next chapter.

"Because he believes in himself, he doesn't try to convince others. Because he is content with himself, he doesn't need others' approval. Because he accepts himself, the whole world accepts him."

Lao Tzu

Mind Maintenance

To help you stay with this feeling of self-acceptance, I'd like you to do the following every day for a week:

Meditate: Take a few minutes to connect to your breath by simply saying calm on the in-breath and relax on the out-breath.

Reflect: Start to reflect on the following sentence: I allow myself to observe the situation without judgement so that I can evolve and I am ready to accept what is.

Journal: Bring your thoughts to a place of evaluation. Remember as you write down what came to mind, you don't need to judge. It is what it is. Doing this exercise every day is helpful because you will slowly, over a few weeks, start to become more aware of your own behaviour and notice things you are not aware you were doing.

Another really important part of self-acceptance is to be kind to yourself, which we will look at in the next chapters. So let's meet in Self-Love where we are going to practise falling madly and unconditionally in love with ourselves. Sound fun? It is! Let's go!

3

SELF-LOVE

One thing I know for sure is that it doesn't matter how successful you are, how much money you are making, how strong you are, whether you are a man or a woman, self-love is for everyone. Loving yourself is not reserved for a select few, but something we *all* deserve. You, yes you, deserve to be loved. If you feel a void within, if you have been searching outside of yourself for ways to feel love, if you have ever doubted whether you are *enough* and whether you are *loved*, it's time to go to the mind gym. Let's exercise the love muscle now and create a clear pathway between your mind and your heart.

In this chapter we are going to celebrate YOU. I want you to switch your focus from whoever or whatever has been draining you or upsetting you, and allow yourself to focus fully on how magical and wonderful you are. Think of it like that moment on an aeroplane when the aircrew tells you to put on your own oxygen mask before attending to your child. It feels selfish, but it makes total sense – you can't help anyone if you are dead! It is time to ignite the love within you, fill up your love cup and let it overflow – there will be so much love, you'll be able to spread it far and wide. The way you love yourself affects all aspects of your life, not just romantic relationships. It can affect your friendships, your career, your body image. The need to search for validation outside of yourself and settling for less then you actually want all changes when you truly love yourself.

"To acquire love, fill yourself up with it until you become a magnet."

Charles F. Haanel

Simple changes

I've been looking forward to writing this chapter for months and in order to do so, and ensure I walk the walk, I've even done a bit of a spring clean of my own self-love practice. It's just like your wardrobe – once in a while it needs a good old declutter and tidy up. I've added my favourite loving kindness meditation to my daily schedule and even recorded a new version of it to send to all my clients and friends. And, of course, I'm going to share it with you too. Upping your self-love practice doesn't have to be complicated – for example, it can be as simple as changing the way you speak about yourself to others, and to yourself, as you'll discover in the positive affirmation exercise; moving on from a friendship that's draining you, as you start to truly value yourself; and knowing you are enough, as you'll see when you get to the being enough and love letter exercises later on. You'll find plenty of exercises in this chapter to help you work out a self-love practice that works for you and I'm so excited about the benefits I know it's going to bring to you!

Soothing ourselves

I believe that as a society we have never needed self-love and self-care as much as we do now. People are under so much stress with the pace of life, juggling careers and home lives, not to mention the pressure placed on us by social media

A HEALTHY LOVE!

You might be wondering how loving yourself really affects you. Well, I can tell you that it has a *huge* impact on you, not just mentally but physically. Loving yourself and, as a result, having high self-esteem do more than make you feel good in the moment. Psychologist Andy Martens, and his colleagues at the University of Canterbury, New Zealand, have shown that loving ourselves and having high self-esteem actually have huge health benefits by protecting our heart and immune system. In their research study they found that people with higher self-esteem had a higher cardiac vagal tone, meaning their parasympathetic nervous system, which slows down and calms the heart, is more active (see a great exercise on pages 162–3 to help you to stimulate the vagus nerve as part of your self-care routine).

Kristin Neff, author and Associate Professor at the University of Texas, believes that self-compassion supports us positively and that, conversely, self-criticism activates our sympathetic nervous system, also know as "fight or flight". This increases stress hormones such as cortisol in the bloodstream – a hormone that has been labelled by the press as "public enemy number 1".

Acknowledging these health effects and knowing how our words and actions can affect our mind and bodies, it is surprising that we still at times resist speaking positively, thinking good thoughts and loving ourselves.

and our high-tech lives. "I'm overwhelmed" is probably the concern I hear the most in my practice. At times I feel that too and those are the days that I meditate twice as much. Self-love and self-care are what we need to soothe ourselves.

Many of my clients, no matter how successful they are professionally, lack something in their personal lives and that something is love, especially self-love. I've seen the most powerful and strong business people moved to tears (even those who tell me they never cry) when I have simply asked them to put their hands over their hearts and then say something nice to themselves, like "I've got this" or "I'm doing the best I can and that's enough." It seems so crazy to think that we would say such things to our friends all the time, yet neglect saying them to ourselves.

So throughout this chapter I want to share with you some of the most powerful tools, which I use with my clients and for myself, to awaken your self-love. To love yourself is your birthright, it's within you, but it may take some practice to become really good at it and that's okay. With the toolbox I've created for you, in time loving yourself will become second nature.

YOUR TOOLBOX: WHAT DO YOU BELIEVE ABOUT YOURSELF?

Before we dive in deeper, I would like you to answer the questions below. I'm asking them now as I know that the answers will bring to the surface the wounds within that need the most love and healing. I am, however, aware that the questions are challenging, perhaps requiring you to confront deeply buried feelings, so if you feel it's too difficult to answer them now, come back to them when the time feels right for you. It may help to have your journal to hand (see page 6) to help you explore your answers and feelings further.

1. Do you believe you are lovable?
   I'm lovable because….
2. Do you believe sometimes you are unlovable?
   If yes, what makes you believe this?
      Now, finish this sentence: I deserve to be loved because…
3. Is there anything standing in your way of loving yourself? If yes, what is it?

If you feel that you are unlovable, let's take a look at what you have written. Are they actual facts about yourself or just things you have come to believe to be true over time? As children when we feel ugly, or dumb or not enough, our parents are quick to correct us and remind us that we are beautiful inside and out, smart and more than enough. Of course, sadly this isn't true for everyone. Some people's negative feelings about themselves come from the people closest to them.

The good news is that as adults we have the power to turn the unlovable part into lovable. YOU have that power to start loving yourself and believing that you are LOVABLE for sure! As Rick Hanson says in his book *Buddha's Brain*, "You're giving yourself today the caring and encouragement you should have received as a child, but perhaps didn't get in full measure." And little by little you will begin to give yourself that love as you take time to work through the self-love exercises and take care of you.

Loving myself

My mum taught me to love and respect myself, but later in life I realized that I had spent a lot of my adult life looking for love outside of myself. I used to love the phrase "you complete me", until I kept finding myself in relationships that didn't really complete me at all. It took me losing my sense of who I was in a relationship before I truly was able to come home to me, and love myself the way I wanted someone else to love me.

Being back on the dating scene in my 30s and not knowing how that whole thing worked, really pushed me to stop and look at my love relationship with myself. I think back then I had actually been running from it because I didn't want to face it, so I didn't spend much time alone. I kind of feared being alone or ending up alone. It was during this time I learnt what it meant to really love and respect myself. As my love for myself grew, I started to respect myself more in every relationship and stopped being worried about whether my approach to each relationship was the right one. When I started to realize that what I was seeing in other people, good or bad, was my own reflection I started to make other choices for myself.

I became so aware of my patterns, and my strengths and weaknesses – the things I loved and the things I wanted to improve on within myself. It became obvious to me that if I was not settled within, and if I didn't really know who I truly was, that was exactly what I would attract in the other person. I remember being in a relationship that was pretty happy, but behaving in a jealous way (without good reason). As much as I tried not to feel jealous, it kept happening. It was super unflattering and really out of character for me and how I actually believed a relationship should be. I realized I had dragged my past of hurt and disappointment into that relationship and I was projecting my insecurity in a really ugly way.

I knew I had some work to do within myself to be able to trust someone again and that started with loving myself and knowing that I am enough no matter what happens to me, so I left the relationship and began to really work on building my self-love. Thank goodness I did because the next relationship I had was with my now husband and throughout our 10 years together we have had to spend a lot of time apart. I cannot imagine how that would have ever succeeded if I had not worked on my wounds and made the decision to trust and love with an open heart again – being jealous on our busy schedules would have been a disaster.

What are you searching for?

If you want to align yourself with attracting relationships that feel good, where there is mutual respect and joy, your mission needs to be to work on your self-love. Imagine all of the energy you waste looking for those things outside of yourself – now you can spend that time on you. If you are willing to invest in being in a relationship to love someone else, surely you can start by giving yourself some of that support, love, strength and care. Once you start to believe that all relationships are mirrors reflecting back the healed and the unhealed within you, working on yourself suddenly becomes very attractive. As you probably know exactly what it is you would like to attract.

As I shared with you above, in the past I have been guilty of searching for happiness and love outside of myself and really ignoring my own power. I would like you to tune in for a moment and ask yourself: What am I searching for outside of myself? It was a game changer for my own self-love when I realized I am in charge of making myself feel loved, safe, heard, strong and confident. The self-compassion practice (see pages 129–30) will support you in this too.

"If you love yourself, you love others. If you hate yourself, you hate others. In relationship with others, the other is nothing but a mirror."

Osho

Keeping an open heart

Many people close their hearts or create an invisible wall after a relationship break-up. They become so frightened of getting their heart broken again that they go from relationship to relationship or settle for someone they know deep down is not right for them, and in the process they end up hurting themselves. This can happen when friendships break down too. When we close our hearts because of hurt or anger, love can't flow in or out and even our own self-love gets suffocated. My husband and I had both had our hearts broken, and I'll never forget the day we looked each other in the eyes and agreed that we were in deep trouble. We knew we had both opened our hearts fully and if it wasn't going to last it was going to hurt. We both jumped in and committed to our relationship that day and invested emotionally as two equals.

I have come to believe that when we are brave we get rewarded. When we are willing to open our hearts to love fully we open ourselves up to the possibility that we might get hurt, but we also open up to the possibility that we may love and be loved beyond our wildest dreams. If we are not willing to risk anything, chances are like anything else in life the return probably won't be great. I believe we will attract what we are willing to give.

Hypnotherapist Marisa Peer explains how important it is to not carry the hurt with us, but express it as soon as we can. She says that when we are balanced we are able to say to the person, "You hurt my feelings when you…" By doing so we let it go so it doesn't fester in our body and we are able to open our hearts again.

You are enough

One of the most fundamental things in our lives – I think of it as the foundation our lives are built on – is to know that no matter what has happened to you in life you are 100 per cent enough, always enough. When you can say, "I am enough", and truly mean it, you are well on your journey to loving yourself. We are all born enough, but somehow through life this belief is challenged. If there are areas of your life where you are not feeling enough, the chances are that this belief was created when you were a child and it's lingering in your unconscious mind. There are many different situations that can make a child feel they are not enough. Examples might be being bullied or your parents getting divorced and one parent leaving you behind to start another family. You might have felt "Why me?", "Aren't I enough for you?" and from that moment the feeling of not being enough was created. Many of my clients ask me to do hypnosis with them to explore why they feel this way.

"I am enough" seems like such a simple statement, but these three words are far from simple. They are very powerful and when we can say them to ourselves and about ourselves, and really believe them to be true, we feel empowered and can more easily love ourselves. Feeling that you are enough solves lots of situations. For example, when we don't feel we are enough we take it personally when someone comments on our work or something we have created. When we feel we are enough, we are able to see the comment as just someone's else perspective and not think "I'm useless" or "I'm worthless" or "They don't like me." Feeling you are enough means you know that their opinion about you, or what you have made or created, does not define who you are because you are enough.

YOUR TOOLBOX: ARE YOU ENOUGH?

Go through the list below and write down from 1–10 where you are on the scale of feeling good enough, where 1 is "not enough" and 10 is "knowing I'm always enough".

- Relationship (use different relationships here that are challenging you)
- Love and family
- Body
- Money
- Career
- When being criticized

This will give you an indication of what you need to work on and reinforce daily in your affirmations. When feeling enough is between 7–10, you are less likely to take things personally and fewer things will trigger you or make you doubt yourself. You will more easily set boundaries for yourself and strive for the things you want rather than settle for less. If you're at the lower end of the scale, moving up will help you to feel more empowered and be able to communicate and act from a place of knowing your worth. Be reassured that no matter how low you are on the scale, you can move up by working on your self-love and by doing the exercises in this chapter and the other chapters. I have created a positive self-love meditation for you to help you feel enough at all times. You can listen to it as often as you need to – just head to www.zenme.tv/mindtools. See pages 135–8 for the positive effect this meditation has had on my client Clint's life and career.

In this meditation I encourage you to take 5 minutes for yourself to close your eyes and create some positive affirmations by repeating the words silently in your mind "I am", saying "I" on the in-breath and "am" on the out-breath, then add whichever positive words support you best in this moment, such as:

- Enough
- Confident
- Lovable
- Strong
- Happy
- Love
- Calm

I encourage you to repeat "I am enough" on its own for at least a couple of minutes as you feel the rhythm of the words and your breath merge, before adding the words of your choice. You can switch it up too and say the words out loud if that feels comfortable to you. If you are working on moving up the scale of feeling enough, I suggest doing this meditation daily.

Sarah's story

My client Sarah had been dating a guy for a year and desperately wanted the relationship to move onto the next level. At the same time she would often complain about the way he spoke to her disrespectfully and his lack of communication whenever it suited him – he was always leaving her hanging, while she waited for him to get in touch. She had fallen for him and told herself, and me, that he was the one, even if there were things about his behaviour she did not agree with. She would even make excuses and defend his poor behaviour at times.

When I asked her how it made her feel when he treated her this way and what she really wanted to say to him, she said she felt disrespected, doubted herself and felt that she was not good enough. She really wanted to tell him that his behaviour was not okay, but she was afraid that if she did he would break up with her. I asked her to reflect back over her life and notice if there were other times when she had felt this way. She said that when she was a child she felt that her parents didn't have time for her and they left her on her own a lot or with different nannies or family members. It made her feel as if she was not a priority, not worthy of their time or love and not important to them. Looking back over that situation she became aware that his behaviour was a familiar pattern being played back to her and although she knew how to cope with it because the situation was similar to her childhood dynamics, it wasn't what she ultimately wanted from a relationship. She also understood now that it wasn't that her parents didn't care about her; they were doing what they thought best by providing a steady income and good schooling, which meant them being away from home and her. Later she also discovered they had their own relationship difficulties, which helped her accept that they did what they could from what they knew and their limitations. This is often the case – parents do the best they can given their conditioning through childhood and their circumstances. It may not be what you would have done or what you find acceptable, but it can help to understand it from a different perspective.

I asked her what she would advise her best friend to do in the same circumstances. She said, "I would tell her to know her worth, respect herself and know that she is 100 per cent enough and deserves someone who sees that and loves her the way she loves them." I asked her if she was willing to accept that advice for herself. It took a moment and a lot of tears before she said, "I'm going to work on loving myself and I don't want a relationship until I'm ready to go into one knowing I am enough." I was extremely proud of her coming to this conclusion and excited to watch her blossom on her self-love journey. What catapulted Sarah to look at her wounds was a romantic relationship, but the same conclusion could have been reached through any type of relationship. It is not so much about the relationship or the challenge, but more about what it brings to the surface to be acknowledged and healed.

YOUR TOOLBOX:
BE YOUR OWN BEST FRIEND

Take a current relationship or situation you are struggling with and write down what advice you would give your best friend in the same circumstances.

Now read it back and ask yourself, "Am I willing to take that advice for myself?" I bet you just gave yourself the best advice ever!

If you answered no to taking the advice, why was that?
What will happen if you take the advice?
What will happen if you don't?

This really is the essence of self-love. Taking the time to care for yourself, and be kind and forgiving to yourself, in the way you would with your own best friend.

Withholding love

If someone withheld love from you as a child, you may withhold love yourself or have become a needy adult – perhaps you have become fixated on wanting love from a particular person and, as a result, you've been willing to accept crumbs. Let's just unravel this for a moment. Let's say your parent didn't show you that love because they didn't love themselves, that because of their own conditioning they didn't know how to give that love to someone. Have you ever considered that? Often when we understand that person's full conditioning, how they were raised, their limitations, we start to understand the reason why that person wasn't able to give us what we needed emotionally, why they only gave us "crumbs". I like the analogy of accepting crumbs because really I'm sure you deserve the whole cake, and as you fall more and more in love with yourself, you will come to know that too.

And, by the way, what's that person's story, in your life now, who is giving you crumbs? Do they love themselves enough to know how to give love? Are they ready to be in a relationship? Or are you perhaps subconsciously the one who is withholding love because that way you won't get hurt? Are you receiving crumbs because that's all you believe you deserve or because you are only really giving crumbs yourself?

We've all been in situations where we fall out with someone we care about, but both parties are too proud or stubborn to say sorry. Instead we both withhold love from one another, until one of the parties suddenly reaches out and then all is forgotten. The same goes for a situation that is frustrating you beyond belief – you are actually better off sending that situation and the people love rather than anger and hate, even just in your mind, because clearly love is what is needed for it to be resolved, healed or for you to let it go, and sending love rather than negative thoughts will serve you better. It may be that the relationship is beyond repair and that it has caused a lot of hurt and upset, but you will feel a greater peace within when you wish that person well in some way, whether that's by wishing for them to find love within, healing or happiness – in essence, by doing so, you are letting yourself off the hook from needing to hold a grudge against that person. When we hold a grudge, it is only ourselves that we hurt.

"Withholding love is a form of self-sabotage, as what we withheld from others, we are withholding from ourselves."
Marianne Williamson

YOUR TOOLBOX: IGNITE THE LOVE

Take a moment to ask yourself if you are withholding love from yourself or in the relationship that is challenging you? Use your journal to explore these feelings if you need to.

Ask yourself:

- Am I withholding love?
- Why am I withholding love?
- How is withholding love serving me?
- Where do I need to redirect my love to?
- What can I focus on that will make me feel more love?
- How would letting go and letting love flow serve me?

Become your own thought detective

To truly know your own worth you have to be willing to start celebrating yourself, stop putting yourself down and stop comparing yourself to others. I want you to learn to be your own thought detective. Start to notice how you are feeling in different situations during the day, especially the moments that challenge your self-worth. It can also help to write your feelings down on your phone or in your journal. What were you doing in that moment? Who were you speaking to and so on? When you notice your sense of self-worth switching, notice what it is triggering in you and try to change your actions and switch to focusing on having a more compassionate mindset in that moment.

If you know hanging out with certain people is going to make you feel crap, why are you doing it? Is that what loving yourself looks like? No! If you are following certain people online and they make you feel awful about yourself, unfollow! At the dreaded annual company or family party when that one person corners you and you can feel they are dumping on you and making you feel bad, have an excuse up your sleeve and politely finish the conversation and move along. You do not have to stay and listen and be dumped on emotionally and verbally if you don't want to, just to avoid upsetting someone and at the expense of your wellbeing.

Knowing your worth is also about having the courage to choose relationships that are going to lift you up. Be confident that if you pass on a relationship or move on from someone another one that is better aligned with you will appear. When you know your worth you stop comparing yourself to others and putting yourself down and you start choosing relationships and the company of people that lift you and light you up. See pages 89–90 for a great exercise that helps you cut the cord with negative people in your life.

Reframing with positive affirmations will support your self-love and self-worth journey and it's a tool you can use all day long. By the end of the chapter I'm hoping you will be a reframe champion!

YOUR TOOLBOX:
REFRAME – WHAT IS AND ISN'T TRUE
ABOUT WHAT YOU THINK OF YOURSELF?

As I touched on in Self-Awareness, the way you speak to yourself can either build you up or tear you down. It's time to get in the driving seat of your self-talk and start taking the route that will not just lift you up but lead you to your ideal relationship and support you in finding inner peace. After all, how can we learn to love ourselves if we constantly talk to ourselves in such a negative way?

Jack Canfield, author of *Chicken Soup for the Soul*, says that out of the 60,000–80,000 thoughts we have a day, 80 per cent of them are negative. That's a whole lot of negative self-talk and it's crazy to think that we would do that to ourselves. He also says, "When we think something is possible, we're more likely to make the effort to achieve it. If we think it's impossible, we won't bother trying." And Jack also confirms what I mentioned on page 100 – that the thoughts we think have an effect on our body. Doesn't that convince you right now to be super selective about how you speak and think about yourself when it comes to yourself and your relationships?

To become an expert at reframing you have to commit consciously to stop yourself in your tracks when you are speaking negatively to yourself and literally reframe there and then. In the beginning you will catch negative thoughts creeping in many times a day, but after a while they will become less frequent and you will be able to reframe more quickly.

Let's start with any false beliefs (see page 43) or negative statements you have created about yourself or the relationships you want to heal. False statements or beliefs are things you have repeated to yourself so often you have come to believe them to be true. But deep down you know that they are not true.

What are they? Write them down. Examples might be:

- I suck at relationships
- I don't feel as if I'm ever enough
- They always leave
- I'll end up alone
- No one ever really sees me
- No one understands me
- Relationships bring out the worst in me

Now rewrite those sentences in ways that are positive and support you.

So "I suck at relationships" would become "I'm great at relationships" and "I don't feel as if I'm ever enough" would become "I know I am enough", and so on.

Reframe as many beliefs as come to mind and make them into empowering statements about yourself. Repeat them every time you catch yourself sliding down the slippery slope of self-loathing and get on with the self-loving instead!

It can help to get support with this, so consider making your empowering statement known to others, maybe your closest friends or by writing it on your mirror, or on a post-it note. I would love to hear and support you in this too, so share it online tagging #INYIM *It's Not You, It's Me.*

Meeting your needs

Time after time my clients tell me they are scared to be honest with their partners about what they need from the relationship. It is really important to have this conversation at the beginning, and that includes for work relationships too. If we fail to communicate what we want, for fear of losing the relationship, our needs won't be met and we risk losing ourselves – we shrink to fit and that will cause its own pain and frustration, leading to both physical and emotional problems.

"If you communicate one thing but want another, it's incongruent. No one is going to read your mind. If you want something you are going to have to ask for it."

Self-love leads to higher self-esteem and as a result your needs are more likely to be met in a relationship. When your love for yourself and your self-esteem is high it becomes logical and totally okay for you to communicate your needs in any relationship.

You will ask for what you want in an authentic, assertive and confident way rather than being needy and fearful of the outcome and you will be able to move on more easily if the needs you have communicated are not accepted.

YOUR TOOLBOX: WORKING OUT YOUR NEEDS

Try answering the following questions to gain some clarity about your needs:

In this relationship what do I
- Need? ....
- Give? ....
- Want to give? ....
- Receive? ....
- Want to receive? ....

You might find that there is a discrepancy between what you are receiving and what you want to receive, and what you are giving and what you want to give. Answering these questions should help you to clarify where you need to put the work in to make sure it is all aligned with what you deserve when you look at it from a perspective of loving yourself.

Do remember, though, that it is okay to compromise and negotiate at times as long as the relationship is balanced and it feels good to you. It's also important to be open to receiving love in different ways as we all have different communication styles. Let me give you an example: you may have been raised to believe that love and affection are shown in material ways. However, your partner may believe "it's the thought that counts" and show love by giving you something of a sentimental rather than a monetary value, or perhaps he or she believes actions speak louder than words and they like cooking for you, driving you around or even doing the housework. It's important to understand how your partner perceives these things too, so they can feel that what they do is also a valid way of showing love.

YOUR TOOLBOX: A LOVE LETTER TO YOURSELF

Writing a love letter to someone we really love is pretty easy, so how come it can be so hard and almost silly to write one to ourselves? As easy as it can be to say nice things to others and compliment them, it can be difficult to say them to yourself. Yet it is so important because your opinion of yourself matters, it matters more than anyone else's.

In this letter you are going to tell yourself all the nice things you would like someone else to tell you, but it's going to mean even more because this is a true act of self-love and because we both know it doesn't matter what other people tell us unless we believe it ourselves. No matter how cute or charming someone else thinks you are, you are not really going to acknowledge and accept the compliment unless you believe it to be true yourself. This is why relying on outside validation is not sustainable.

Keep the letter simple. You can either make it specific to a current situation in your life or more generally about loving yourself. As an example, below are some of the words I like to use in love letters to myself. OMG I can't believe I actually just wrote those words – it has been a journey getting there but I can tell you it feels good to say "the words I like to use in love letters to myself". Get creative below and write the most loving letter to yourself you have ever written. This experience is for you so make it an act of self-love. Sit somewhere relaxing, make your favourite drink (mine is a matcha tea or coffee) and play your favourite tune. (I'm obsessed with "Weightless" by Marconi Union – backed by neuroscience, it's written specifically to calm the mind. I feel it helps me relax and let the words flow. I wrote this whole book listening to it!)

Dear Me or write your name (whichever feels best to you)
  I'm so proud of you for how you are being disciplined with your self-compassion practice and making time for it every day. I want you to know that you are always loved and supported even in the moments when you feel alone. Always know you are infinite love and light. You are always enough!

And so on…

Another example might be to write how proud you are of yourself for handling a situation the way you did or to tell yourself that even though you are feeling hurt and sad at the moment, know that you are loved and that it will pass, that you are a really amazing human being and that the world needs you.

You can be as creative as you like – after all, this is *your* love letter. Mention as many nice things you can think of about yourself and really notice how you feel as you are writing the letter – really allow yourself to feel each word. You can read it back to yourself if you want to – it's really powerful to read it aloud and I have had clients who have read it to themselves in the mirror, to me or even to their partner. Do whatever works best for you.

"If I love myself I love you, If I love you, I love myself."

Rumi

YOUR TOOLBOX:
IN THE MIRROR

In Louise Hay's book *Mirror Work* she says "Doing mirror work is one of the most loving gifts you can give yourself" and I totally agree. Something magical happens once we let the awkwardness of it fall away, when it's just you staring back at you, completely authentically, ready to have the courage to speak lovingly to yourself. It can be a little uncomfortable, yes, for most of us, but it's also so intimate and can be a great way to send yourself a loving message, and accept and love yourself as you are. And hopefully you are getting more and more used to it.

I have watched many clients stand in front of the mirror in my office looking as nervous as if they were going on a first date. Then over a few sessions I've witnessed them becoming more comfortable as they stand taller and move through the different stages from saying statements such as "I hate myself", "I don't like my body" to "I think I can like myself", "I want to like myself" to "I like myself" and then "I love myself and my body." To watch them literally switch on their lights within, and the joy on their faces as they become more and more comfortable in their own body, is amazing.

On page 40, in Self-Awareness, I asked you to look in the mirror and write down the words that were coming to mind. Perhaps back then there were a few not so supportive words you wrote down. The purpose of this exercise is so that ultimately, after a while, you'll be able to look yourself straight in the eye and say, "I love you", and really feel that love you have for yourself.

I'm not expecting it to happen overnight, although if it does that's awesome, but I can tell you I'm pretty confident you will feel really proud of yourself when it happens and that it feels good. It's okay to start saying it too before you believe it, as with time you will come to believe it. Once you have been able to do that, you will be able to catch yourself quicker and redirect your mind whenever it drifts to old behaviour and the negative thoughts creep in, and you will start to feel strong and comfortable in situations where you didn't before.

This exercise can be done very easily in the mornings as you are brushing your teeth or drying your hair. Stand in front of the mirror and try out some of the positive affirmations below to find the right starting point for you, knowing that you will be gradually moving towards loving yourself.

- I like myself
- I like myself more and more every day
- I love myself
- I like xyz about myself
- I love xyz about myself
- I love my body
- I appreciate my body
- I speak positively about and to myself

Whether you practise one sentence a day, or simply look at yourself in the morning in the mirror and say "morning gorgeous" to yourself, it will help you to build your self-love. Remember I told you already, you deserve this love.

Body image

I've had many clients who struggle with body image issues. By the time I see them they have often tried all sorts of diets, abused their bodies and each time ended up back in the same place because the root cause is still there lingering in their subconscious. And that is not going to be conquered by any diet – only with LOVE.

"I stopped waiting for you to see it, I stopped waiting for you to say it, And I just looked myself in the mirror and said, I LOVE YOU."

Falling in love with our bodies can be hard. Many of us have a skewed idea of what we look like and are constantly striving to perfect our bodies and looks. However, no amount of looking good is going to make you feel good if you don't love what's inside of you. You will be striving for perfection, the unreachable, and there will always be something that will catch your attention that you are not going to like. That's why Simone's story struck a chord with me…

In New Zealand earlier this year, I went to the launch of Simone Anderson's book *Journey to Health*. It was an inspiring and heartfelt evening. I read in an article she had described "her health to be at stake" before she started her weight-loss journey and that her relationship with food was one where "food brought her happiness". Simone became an Instagram sensation for documenting her very honest weight-loss story, inspired many and built a strong following. She lost 194lb in a year, but no matter how amazing that is, it was something else about her story that really touched me that evening.

At the launch I remember her mother saying that her daughter's weight-loss journey had "started with her deciding to love herself". That to me was everything. Right there, that's it, guys, that's where healing starts by loving ourselves right here where we are, not where we are going

"It's quite simple, when you love yourself you make different choices for yourself."

to be. By meeting our own needs, soothing ourselves and treating ourselves lovingly just the way we all deserve. Simone said she actually chose to love her excess skin before deciding to have surgery to remove it.

A diet might sometimes feel like a quick solution, but it's not the long-term answer that's going to make you feel good in your body at all times – that happens only when we choose to LOVE LOVE LOVE ourselves. Every shape is beautiful and it's far more important to focus on being healthy and to learn to accept and love yourself than what diet to try next.

I truly believe that when we love and respect ourselves we become unafraid of showing up in the world the way we were born to show up.

Bernadette's story

"A friend gave me Camilla's number and said, "Call this Life Coach. I think she's perfect for you." I was looking to work with a coach that understood how to boost confidence and give me mind tools I could use in my career and sports. As I was putting Camilla's phone number in my phone, I dialled her by mistake and she happened to pick up as she was driving. I was planning to call her in a few weeks, but when she picked up something told me it was meant to be and I had to book in immediately.

Never in a million years did I know when I started working with her two years ago, to gain more confidence, that I would be going on an inward journey that would prepare me for the toughest year of my life. It was a year when some of my most precious relationships got challenged and a lot of the year was spent in different hospitals visiting my dearest. In one year I almost lost my brother just before we lost both my dad and then my mother. It was a year I would not wish upon anyone – so extremely emotional, sad and exhausting.

Thank goodness I had carried on working on myself with Camilla. We worked on different subtle wounds hidden in my subconscious and the importance of self-love and self-care, and the importance of having a deeper connection with the breath.

I honestly don't know how I would have gotten through this time without the mindful tools Camilla gave me. With so much going on around you, it's easy to get caught up and neglect yourself and I was close at times, but Camilla would remind me that then I was no good to anyone. I needed to look after myself, sleep, meditate and eat well. Being able to pick myself up and centre myself helped me beyond belief.

I wasn't just able to show up fully for myself, but I was able be there for my parents when they needed me the most and also be there for my siblings. I can't believe it took such a life-challenging situation for me to truly know that loving yourself and knowing your worth and that you are enough really is so vital in life in whatever you are going through, and that really helps you make choices in life that are aligned with that even in the most difficult times."

What we can learn from Bernadette's situation is that self-love sees us through even the roughest of rides. With self-love comes resilience and inner strength to carry on in the moments where we feel like we can't.

Self-compassion and your heart

Self-compassion is important to boost self-love. It means to be compassionate to ourselves whether things are going well or not, and it means being able to forgive ourselves when things are tough. It means meeting yourself exactly where you are at and knowing that you matter in this world and that you are lovable.

This exercise is an alternative to the traditional mindfulness-based loving kindness meditation, a practice I urge you to make your best friend. It's impossible really to talk about love and then not talk about our powerful hearts (we've already looked at how everything is vibration on page 33). One of the things I have learnt by studying and teaching the chakras, or energy fields, in the body (see page 148), is that we often try to "work things out logically" in our minds and are completely disconnected from the feelings in our heart. When all we have to do is listen to how we feel to find the answers. There is an excellent saying I try to live by that goes "You know the truth by how it makes you feel". However, sometimes we ignore this because it's not what we want to be feeling and if we act on it, it won't lead us towards the outcome we think we want in that moment. So we ignore how we feel and stay figuring it out in our minds.

When we drop into our hearts this beautiful feeling area, we are able to connect to a powerful source of energy. In her book *High on Heart* my dear colleague Jessie May Wolfe explains the power of our hearts: "Your heart's electromagnetic field holds enough power to light up a small city." Some will even say there is a "heart brain". I have experienced many profound moments with my clients where they have allowed themselves to drop out of their thoughts and logical minds – away from the "should", "must" statements – and into the feeling and the guidance in their hearts. It's often like a light-bulb moment – suddenly they know exactly what feels right to them and what they need to do.

Knowing what I know now about self-compassion, having studied and taught different mindfulness practices and truly understood the benefits of having a daily self-compassion practice, it's beyond me why we aren't all taught this at school. In one of my favourite books, *The Self-Compassion Skills Workbook,* Tim Desmond explains how the brain has a care circuit, which creates the experience of compassion, warmth and love. And with compassion training this can actually grow in size. When it's activated through self-compassion, it can reduce every form of emotional distress, including anxiety, anger and depression. It's a powerful practice and one that has seen many of my clients through difficult times and supported them through anxiety and stress.

I guess the first couple of times I was encouraged to put my hands over my heart and say something kind or loving to myself, I didn't really understand how powerful a practice it actually is, but it didn't take long to feel the difference it was making to my life and my clients.

YOUR TOOLBOX:
SELF-COMPASSION AND YOU

Now try this wonderful self-compassion practice for yourself.

1. Find somewhere comfortable to sit and close your eyes. Place your hands over your heart.
2. Consider first a relationship or situation in your life about which you have been negative or hard on yourself. Let the feelings around this arrive in your mind.
3. Then say: "I'm going to be kind to myself" and repeat the words:
   - May I be safe
   - May I be loved
   - May I be well
   - May I be kind to myself

   Repeat each sentence three times, then switch to saying:
   - I am safe
   - I am love

- I am well
- I am kind to myself

Repeat three times, then add your own nurturing and loving sentence. This can change each time. It could be something along the lines of:

- I am connected to the infinite love in this world
- Love flows through me in abundance
- My heart is open for love to flow in and out in perfect harmony
- I attract loving relationships because I am love
- I am always guided and supported

Sit for as long as you need and, like with any of the other meditations I suggest, feel free to have your favourite relaxing piece of music on or the sound of the ocean playing in the background, or just sit in silence if you prefer – whatever works for you.

YOUR TOOLBOX:
CREATE A SELF-LOVE RITUAL

To get you into the flow of focusing on loving yourself, what's one thing you could do every day to show yourself love? Ask yourself what emotional support you can give yourself today? For example, "Today I will focus on making myself feel good by tapping into my joy, my intuition."

Part of my self-love ritual is to put away my phone 30 minutes to an hour before I go to sleep on weekdays and 2–3 hours before at weekends. I leave it charging far enough away that I would have to get out of bed to reach it, sometimes in another room. This is my way of ending each day by saying because I love myself I give myself the best possible way of resting without stress arriving into my sacred space. Sleep is such a healing time and allowing ourselves enough time to sleep is a sign of self-love too.

I also buy myself flowers because I deserve them. I love the whole ritual behind flowers and caring for them. Whenever I see the flowers at home it just says "I love you" to me and, although I'm married, it reminds me that I am completely capable of meeting my own needs in love too. I did this for myself when I was single and I do it still because it's a loving act that makes me smile. The upside is my husband gets to enjoy them too, as do clients and friends who visit, which shows the ripple effect that a loving act has.

What is the one thing you are going to do as your daily, weekly or monthly ritual of self-love?

YOUR TOOLBOX:
HYPNOTIC VISUALIZATION –
FALLING IN LOVE WITH MYSELF

In this visualization I will guide you on a journey where you will explore and remember all the beauty, wisdom and qualities already within you and imagine yourself fully loving yourself. I have created a special visualization for you to listen to at www.zenme.tv/mindtools.

To give you a taster of what to expect, the visualization starts with closing your eyes and imagining you are opening up a magical box of treasures within. Each piece of beauty you find in this box is another part of you that you love or are proud of. It can be any quality from being a good listener, being kind, having beautiful eyes, having the courage to be authentic or to speak your truth, and so on. It will let your imagination work for you, helping you unlock the treasure of self-love.

Mind Maintenance

To help you stay with this feeling of self-love, I'd like you to do the following every day for a week:

Meditate: Take a few minutes to connect to your breath by simply observing how the breath is flowing through the body.

Reflect: Start to reflect on the following sentence: I choose to love myself because I am love.

Journal: Write down what came to mind, without judging it. Perhaps even acknowledging how your love for yourself has improved from when you started this chapter to now. Even just being open to the idea is movement in a positive direction that will support you.

So I hope you're feeling fulfilled and enriched by a feeling of self-love. I'm now going to show you how to maintain that and take good care of yourself. See you in the next chapter.

4

SELF-CARE

This is huge! I mean as important as self-love. I kind of consider them best friends, they totally go hand in hand. However, just like self-love, self-care is one of those things that gets tossed aside until we find ourselves in a place of feeling rough, stuck or exhausted, or worse we find ourselves in the midst of a panic attack or burnout, then we suddenly wake up and think "Oops, I think I should have looked after myself." I've totally been there too. I'm still slightly puzzled by my younger self, who I think didn't look after herself in the way she deserved to. Seriously, though, we have this one life and if we don't take care of ourselves, our mind and body will start acting out in different ways that really aren't good for us.

Self-care is suddenly this trendy concept we see in magazines, as if it's some elaborate thing we should do for ourselves. Let's get real, guys, self-care is not a luxury, it's your birthright and an absolute *must* if you really want to live a happy, fulfilled life with rewarding relationships. It's so easy to neglect yourself when your focus becomes the needs and feelings of your partner, your children, your job, but when you start to suffer so will all your relationships. So just like anything else in life, and as we've seen throughout this book, it all starts with you.

I'm going to show you how to declutter your life from all the crap you don't need to waste your energy on and help you figure out how to make self-care part of your day-to-day routine. You will soon reap the rewards once you see how looking after yourself improves your relationship with yourself and others.

A self-care plan

I'm going to share my absolute favourite tools with you, some of which I've used for over a decade. I've handpicked tried-and-tested self-care exercises that have seen my clients and me through every scenario you can imagine, and I've created a 7-day easy-to-follow self-care plan to help you get started. After doing that, you can pick and choose the tools that work best for you. I want you to be able to return to the plan again and again whenever you feel like you need a reset, or just need to feel cared for, and be reminded that it's totally fine to take time for you! If you're worried about finding the time, don't be. Most of the exercises only take a few minutes, so there really is no excuse not to make time to care a little more about yourself, right?

Clint's story

Before we get into the exercises, I want to share a real-life story with you, one that sums up perfectly how when we look after ourselves everything else falls into place.

When I thought of asking Clint, a regular student at my class at Unplug Meditation, to talk to me about how self-care had helped him, I was amazed by how far he'd come on that self-care journey in three years. He is now the co-founder of one of Hollywood's most innovative media companies but, like many of us, went through a time of struggling with feeling okay within himself. But he dramatically altered the course of his life because he took back his power and gave himself the time and care he deserved. He got in the driver's seat of his relationship with himself and realized that that was where it all had to start if he wanted to make meaningful change in his life. I loved our honest chat and I hope his story will inspire you and many others to take time for self-care and to know the ripple effect and power it can have on your life and relationships. Here's what Clint told me...

"There was a point in my life when I realized that something had to change. I'd started a new job, thinking it would be everything I had ever dreamt of, but I really wasn't enjoying it – far from it, in fact. It was starting to make me someone I'm not. It's a hard thing to focus on the relationship with yourself – it gets buried when you're so busy and you give away so much of your power in the course of a day. It became hard to remember that it was my relationship with myself that was everything, but I was about to find that out. I suddenly found myself feeling totally overwhelmed and I was struggling to find my footing – the job was seriously affecting my mental health. Because I was in an environment at work that didn't suit me, I was in a constant state of feeling "not enough". I needed a new mechanism to cope with the environment. Of course at the time I thought I was the only one feeling like that but I know now that I wasn't.

I found it really helpful when Camilla explained in the meditation class how the negative things we think and say to ourselves affect us. It was a great reminder of this internal dialogue and once I was aware of it I started reframing "not enough" to "I am enough". I realized I had identified getting that job with my success, my own identity. So coming to the realization that it wasn't the right job, definitely not a good fit for me, and that I had to leave was daunting. It felt like an identity loss; it felt horrible and truly sucked, not least because I had a family to look after.

I gave myself three months to figure out what to do next and meditation became my daily act of self-care, my constant. I'm glad I let my friend know how I was feeling as he introduced me to a meditation app and took me to Camilla's class at Unplug Meditation in LA.

I'm also grateful to my wife for understanding the importance of me taking that time for me – this meant everything to me. She said, "Let's take the summer and then see how you feel." Feeling this bad pushed me to look at myself and flush out all the things that didn't work any longer – the old beliefs and habits – and find new ways of doing things. I was the main provider and I just had to figure it out, so giving up was not an option. Instead it was about finding a new way that would serve me and my family. Meditation helped me find my footing and begin to think constructively about how to rebuild my relationship with myself, which created a way to look at my career with fresh eyes. I started to feel different right away.

I remember Camilla doing a meditation in one of her classes that turned out to be critically important to me. It was about planting the seeds of intentions in the garden of opportunity. I have returned to that garden many times since. It became a safe place to go in my mind and a lot of good thoughts and intentions were planted and grew from there. I rebooted my entire life in 2015, as I started to believe that it's your relationship with yourself that is everything. I began to start each day with self-care, which was a workout then meditation and then, and only then, I would figure out what else I needed to do each day. Self-care was how I aligned myself with what was to come next for me. I also learnt the importance of a morning ritual, which I still do to this day.

The beauty of having gone through this time is that I now listen to my mind and body in a way I didn't before. I now have tools I can rely on, such as positive affirmations, breathing exercises and meditation.

I started with self-care and that has helped me develop self-love, although that is still new to me and it takes a constant reminder. Looking back, this was the best thing that ever happened to me. Getting knocked down emotionally led me to find the courage to found my own company and that led to me meeting the business partner I run my company with today. It felt like a deconstruction. And in retrospect it had to happen. I went to the life gym, I guess. I was a high achiever and dependent on other people's validation, thinking I needed it. Now I know the validation starts with me."

MEDITATION AT YOUR FINGERTIPS

Clint was one of the first clients at Unplug Meditation to encourage me to record my meditations so my students could listen to them whenever they needed them. I followed his advice and recorded my first meditation, which was called "I am". Clint told me he has used this meditation daily since. Little did I know back then that years later my meditations would be serving all over the world and that they had over hundreds of thousands of plays through meditation apps like Insight timer and Unplug Meditation. If you'd like to try some out, head to www.zenme.tv.

A common story

Clint's story moved me so much because I know many people have gone through something similar at some point in their lives. That was why I wrote my last book *Reinvent ME,* because I wanted people who needed support through times like that to know they are not alone and that there are tools there to help them.

As an athlete for most of my life, before becoming a Life Coach, I wasn't very good at saying no. I would just power through and, although that has its place in sport and in business at certain times, I headed straight for a burnout aged 35 and learnt my lesson the hard way. So I take self-care very seriously in my own life. It's what I call non-negotiable because I have seen first hand what can happen and the power of prevention. And that is why I love serving my clients as a Life and Mind Coach because I'm passionate about what I teach, and sharing the importance of self-care before it's too late. Some call me their personal mind trainer.

On my last book tour I spoke to many people going through relationship issues and challenging times. I realized, just like Clint, how so many were not looking after themselves. In fact, during stressful and challenging times taking time for self-care was the last thing on their list of priorities when it needed to be the first, mainly because people often considered self-care a kind of extra thing they had to pay for, such as a massage, a spa day or even a holiday. Of course it can be all of those things too, but self-care can just as easily be having a hot bath with no disturbances, a power nap in the afternoon (my absolute fave and how I navigate through my busy schedule most days – well, that and meditation) or an evening to yourself to do exactly what YOU want. It can also be the way you talk to yourself, nurture your thoughts and relationship with yourself and the way you create positive behaviours and habits in your life so that you can show up for yourself in the best possible way.

YOUR TOOLBOX:
MY 7-DAY SELF-CARE PLAN

So now let's get started. I've put together 7 simple, yet effective, exercises, which are all from my personal self-care regime because they totally rock.

I've written it as a 7-day plan to be done on consecutive days, but please create the plan that works best for you, even if that means repeating the same exercise 7 days straight. You may be drawn to certain exercises and find they fit in with your day better, and that's fine. The main goal is to get you into the habit of knowing it's okay to take time for YOU every day! I'd especially like you to get into the habit of using the morning ritual daily, though. It's such a simple, but powerful, self-care tool.

DAY 1:
MORNING RITUAL

I believe 100 per cent that how we start the day, and the intention we set for the day, lays the foundation for how the rest of the day will play out. As you read in Clint's transformational journey (see pages 135–8), a morning ritual was a vital component in him learning to look after his own needs first. If we start the day taking care of ourselves, it's a way of saying to the universe "I respect and take care of myself first," which will have a positive ripple effect on your day. Why would you ever want to invite other people's energy into your energy field before you have checked in with yourself and asked, "How am I feeling today?" Crazy, right?

My morning ritual has become my favourite thing over the last couple of years and the benefits have been out of this world for me personally. Never in a million years did I think that it would affect my day so much that I would even be able to call myself "a morning person". I was always a complete night owl and loved my lie-ins. Partly I thank Mel Robbins' book *The 5 Second Rule* where she explains how we can talk ourselves in or out of something in 5 seconds and how within that time we have to do an action, like actually get out of bed, because when we physically move the brain starts to build a new habit.

This has become the first part of my morning ritual. I literally count 5, 4, 3, 2, 1, as she suggests, and then jump out of bed. It has stopped the feeling of wanting to hit the snooze button and procrastinate about whether I should get up now or in 10 minutes. Plus it has inspired me to go to bed earlier – the ripple effect I'm talking about. You make one change and, boom, other things start to change in a positive way too.

I'm pretty strict now about what "noise" I let into my sacred space in the mornings and I definitely do not pick up my phone and check emails until I have showered and done my positive affirmation meditation. This ensures that I'm centred and ready to interact with others. We can't control others, but we sure can take responsibility for the attitude and energy we bring to people and situations. I do this in the best way I can each day before venturing out into the world and sitting in LA traffic with an attitude or seeing a client and dumping any shitty energy on them.

And, by the way, before you say, "I haven't got time for this ritual," let me stress that it can take as little or as long as you have. You could start by simply taking 10 deep breaths, put the coffee on whilst reminding yourself of everything you have to be grateful for, and then have a shower before you look at a phone or any emails. And if you have kids it may mean setting the alarm for 10–15 minutes before they usually wake up, but I also have clients who swap things around and do their morning self-care after they've dropped the kids at school.

Now it's your turn to decide what your morning ritual looks like. Try to think of three things that you will do for yourself each morning as a sign of self-care before you start taking care of others and checking your phone or computer. It can be as simple as sitting up in bed and taking three deep breaths in and connecting with your own breath; having that cup of coffee in silence before everyone wakes up; or repeating some beautiful affirmations to yourself whilst taking your shower, where you use a few drops of essential oils such as eucalyptus or peppermint for a bit of extra pampering.

Write down your self-care morning ritual.

DAY 2:
FUEL YOUR JOY

I love this exercise so much and I use it whenever I feel bogged down – it will feel like a spring clean of your life. To look after yourself better what are you going to purge in your life?

In her marvellous book, *Spark Joy*, Marie Kondo encourages us all to look at each piece of clothing in our wardrobe and ask, "Does it spark joy?" and if the answer is no, thank it and let it go. She is on to something here – it's a wonderful mindful way to look at things and I do something similar with my thoughts, habits and relationships. I encourage you to try it.

Ask yourself these questions:

- Is this igniting the fire in my belly?
- Is this an absolute YES?
- Does this fuel my joy?

If not, say, "I let it go with gratitude and love." Because one thing I know for sure is that we cannot add to an overloaded wardrobe, not the one in our homes or the one in our mind. To invite in new relationships we have to make space, throw out that old sweater that no longer feels good, ie the relationship or thoughts that are draining us, and swap the habits that are not serving us from rising. That, beautiful soul, is self-care!

"If one wishes to know love, one must live love, in action."
Leo Buscaglia

HONESTY FOR GOOD HEALTH

For self-care, it is vital that we are honest with ourselves. What we want, speak and do needs to be in alignment for the happiness to flow. If there is opposition in any of those areas, they will come out as unhappiness or disharmony in an area of our life. I remember asking a client who struggled with insomnia "What's keeping you awake?" She told me how she was no longer happy in her relationship, as she and her partner wanted different things, but she was fearful about breaking up as she enjoyed the lifestyle her partner provided and that would have to change if she left him. I asked her what exactly the relationship provided. She replied "Financial freedom", to which I asked "At what cost?" She replied "Emotionally I feel in prison." So all that time she thought she had freedom she felt in prison emotionally. Those two opposite energies were keeping her awake at night because there was a message that she was denying. She knew if she truly stopped and listened to her intuition or guidance, she would have to go through some discomfort and turmoil to align herself and her lifestyle again. What she was putting out there energetically was that she valued the money more than she valued her own happiness and that was never going to align her with attracting more happiness now, was it? She and her partner broke up not long after because she realized that she deserved to be happy as well as having a good lifestyle, and that she didn't have to settle for one or the other long-term, but just make some adjustments temporarily. Like Phil Stutz and Barry Michels explain in the book *The Tools*, endless possibilities lie outside of your comfort zone on the other side of the pain you need to go through to get there.

DAY 3:
LET THE LOVE FLOW

I love this breath-focused meditation, also known as the Heart Breath. It helps you to drop out of your ever-thinking mind for a moment and connect with the heart. When we connect to the heart, everything seems simpler and it reminds us that there is a kinder more compassionate way through even the most difficult times. Breath by breath you will feel your vibration rise. This exercise is extremely helpful if you feel emotionally blocked and are someone who is in your head a lot trying to work everything out when really what you need is to FEEL what guidance is within you instead. You may also find that it clears hurt, frustration or sadness from a past or current relationship.

Let's ignite the heart energy.

1. Sit somewhere comfortable and close your eyes.
2. Visualize a big bright light surrounding you and beaming through you.
3. Now focus on your breath getting slower, and how it's flowing in and out of your heart.
4. Imagine each breath getting deeper and longer, each breath representing love flowing in and out of the heart.
5. If it feels comfortable to you, you can place your hands over your heart to feel the connection with the body a little deeper and you can also focus on words like "love" on the in-breath and "let go" on the out-breath. However, simply focusing on the expansion and love flowing in and out of the heart is powerful in itself.

Notice how raising your vibration brings new energy to the body, how the light you are imagining shining through you is getting brighter and how the breath is getting deeper.

Go to www.zenme.tv/mindtools for the guided version of this meditation.

DAY 4:
DIVORCE YOUR BAD HABITS

Ditching old habits is a big part of self-care. For about four years now I have been hosting workshops called "Design Your Ideal Partner", helping the participants align themselves emotionally and energetically with what they want to manifest. Because what I had come to realize, both through my own manifestation practice and from my clients, is that when we start behaving in a way that is aligned with what we are manifesting, get clear about how we want to behave and what we specifically want, we are ready to receive. What we don't want is to walk into any relationship with old habits from past relationships lingering. I remember "divorcing" feeling needy in a relationship and creating a habit of feeling comfortable and trusting instead. I also divorced the habit of having my phone on the bedside table and fell in love with leaving it in the kitchen or anywhere out of reach from the bed. It might not only be habits you are divorcing – it could be friendships or even foods you know aren't good for you.

Rewrite the habit you want to divorce now that shows that you take the relationship with yourself and therefore other relationships seriously too.

Say aloud:

"I'm committed to divorce this [habit] to show myself I am putting self-care at the top of my list of priorities and I'm taking my relationship with myself to the next level."

Now write down any other habits/people that have popped into your head that you want to divorce.

And then write what you are inviting in instead.

Go ahead and ask yourself:

To look after me, I'm also divorcing .... today.

Some people have said sugar, coffee and energy-zapping friends. I'm wondering what yours are.

I'm ready to invite .... into my life.

DAY 5:
CHAKRA BALANCING

A long time ago I came across an audio recording from Deepak Chopra of his Chakra Balancing Meditation and it's been on my iTunes ever since. I first used it when I was touring in a UK sell-out play called *Calendar Girls*. I was acting for the first time in my life and in desperate need of some self-care – this exercise became my go to. I fell madly in love with it and still use it weekly.

The chakras represent the 7 main energy fields in the body and they run from the bottom of the spine up through the middle of the body through the belly, solar plexus, chest, throat, the area between your eyebrows and the top of your head. Think of them as spinning wheels of energy in the body, when they are all rotating at the same rate we feel aligned and energized because the pathway is clear for our breath and energy to flow freely through our body. However, when one of the chakras slows down we feel out of alignment and start saying things like "I feel stuck", "Things aren't flowing for me", "I feel blocked" and so on. There are different ways we can align and balance the chakras – I personally use certain yoga exercises as well as the exercise I am about to share with you.

When we go through emotional challenges, we can store some of that trauma and those feelings in our bodies and suddenly the body starts to act out with pain, discomfort, skin problems, even as a disease or a cold. In their book *The Complete Idiot's Guide to Chakras*, Betsy Rippentrop Ph.D. and Eve Adamson explain how your health, both physically and mentally, and the chakras are interlinked on a spiritual level, which can help give you a deeper understanding of yourself. Do, however, always consult a doctor with any health issues. Each chakra represents different types of emotions and feelings we may be holding onto. I love the analogy in *The Essential Guide to Chakras* by Swami Saradananda: "If you block a river by throwing waste into it, its flow is reduced. Similarly, if your body is filled with physical toxins, the flow of prana is inhibited." Prana means universal energy that flows through the body. This makes so much sense and explains why we say we feel stuck or blocked or that things aren't flowing. It could mean you are holding onto past or current emotions and feelings around a relationship or situation. There is also a colour and element connected to each chakra, as I will guide you through in the meditation, and each chakra represents different areas such as confidence, passion and communication.

I have seen incredible shifts in people when I have worked with them on releasing held emotions from relationships. I have seen them let go of stagnant emotions and improve stomach discomfort and digestive issues. I have seen clients walk in so tight chested with anxiety that they were completely disconnected from their breath – once they'd released old emotions of hurt and sadness and forgiven people, they often described becoming balanced as a huge weight being lifted off their chest and sometimes shoulders. Another common one is when clients tune into their throat chakra and finally let go of things they have wanted to say to someone for ages, but never communicated – holding onto it has caused stress and tension in their throat and neck and even affected their immune system.

I have recorded an extended audio version of this meditation for you. Just head to www.zenme. tv/mindtools. If you are ever in LA, check out my events calendar on social media or on my website for any upcoming events, as I regularly guide chakra balancing classes.

Before you begin please get comfortable either on a yoga mat on the floor, couch or bed and at a time when you know you won't get disturbed. Some people like to lie down rather than sitting as you can really become aware of the energy flowing through the body as you balance and cleanse each chakra. You can place your hands over each chakra as we move through them or just relax them down by your side.

If you like to work with crystals, then you can integrate them into this practice, placing them along your body on the energy fields to enhance the meditation. A quick guide to working with crystals is to match the colour of the crystals to the colour of the chakra, so if you happen to have a green crystal at home it goes with your heart chakra, and so on.

Like in any meditation (see page 9), know that your thoughts will come and go and pull you away and that's okay. Let the focus you use to bring you back again and again be the colour of the chakra. You may or may not see the exact colour or any colour at times as everyone visualizes differently and that's totally okay – just know you will go on the journey that is meant for you as you try to imagine each colour in that moment. When it comes to repeating the sentences, it's fine to do so silently but, equally, if it feels right for you to say them aloud then that's great too. You can find what works best for you.

Start by bringing your focus to the 1st Chakra – the Root Chakra based at the bottom of your spine. Colour: red / Element: earth

Imagine the colour red as you connect with this chakra. Notice what you notice as you slowly tune into this area of the body. Are you becoming aware of any tightness, stress or tiredness here to be released?

Sometimes fear can be present in this chakra – fear of changes and what will be, financial worries and concerns about living arrangements, but as you focus on the red colour, letting go of whatever you need to let go of, imagine it floating away with your out-breath into a big bright light and being dissolved. You are allowing for the connection with the earth energy. Imagine that earth energy flowing up through the feet easily and effortlessly and up through this area of the body. You will start to feel more and more grounded, rooted and stable. Repeat the words, "I am safe", three times slowly here before you move up along to the next chakra.

Bring your focus to the 2nd Chakra – the Sacral Chakra – based in the middle of the belly beneath the belly button. Colour: orange / Element: water

Through this chakra you connect to your creativity, passion and inspiration, but if you hold onto emotions from situations that are draining you, this flow could be blocked, leaving you feeling empty, exhausted and even stuck. The aim is to get everything flowing again.

Tune into the orange colour flowing through the belly like water as you notice whether there is anything here blocking your flow, any stagnant energy or emotions you can let go of and let the water cleanse away. The beauty of letting go is that you create space for new energy to flow through you. Nurture and give back to yourself through this area and allow for new ideas to be born through here. As you fully balance this chakra, you ignite and connect to the passion, inspiration and creativity within you. Repeat the words, "Everything in my life flows with ease", slowly three times and then move up along to the 3rd chakra.

Bring your focus to the 3rd Chakra – the Solar Plexus Chakra – based in the solar plexus, in the abdomen above your belly button. Colour: yellow / Element: fire

As you tune in here to the colour yellow or the fire in your solar plexus, notice whether there is any tightness or discomfort in this area. This chakra represents the upper digestive system so ask yourself, "How am I digesting life and situations through here?", or "Is there anything here that is repeating on me?" ie an issue, emotion, relationships, and then just notice what comes to mind. As the element is fire it can feel very powerful to imagine a yellow light shining right through the body here cleansing away any stale energy. Sometimes emotions and feelings of anger, resentment or controlling behaviour can appear to be released. And as you balance this chakra you connect to your confidence and self-belief, turning up your own light allowing you to feel empowered as you let your shoulders fall back and the solar plexus open up for your light to shine brightly. It feels empowering when you visualize yourself standing fully in your own light! Repeat the words, "I am shining my light brightly and I am enough", three times slowly.

Bring your focus to the 4th Chakra – the Heart Chakra, based in the middle of the body next to the heart. Colour: green / Element: air

Tune into the green colour now. This chakra represents all matters of the heart. From this space you can tune into the guidance you are feeling here and also notice if there is anything weighing on your chest making it difficult to breathe easily, and then literally asking yourself, "What am I feeling here?" or if there is a specific situation on your mind you can ask, "How do I feel about it?" The key is to drop into what you're feeling rather than thinking. This chakra is all about feeling everything and allowing all feelings that are no longer serving you to come to the surface to clear. From here you can choose to forgive and let go of issues and emotions like hurt, sadness and grief as you allow for the infinite loving energy to flow through you. Remember, if you are withholding love from a situation, resisting letting it go, you are also withholding love from yourself as love and energy can't flow through a blocked chakra. You forgive to set yourself free, to open yourself up to give love and be loved again. Forgiving someone does not necessarily mean agreeing with their behaviour – it just means you stop it from poisoning you over and over again, carrying it with you into the now. Repeat the words, "I am love", three times slowly (see the exercise Heart Breath on pages 145–6 to work further with the energy field of the heart).

Bring your focus to the 5th Chakra – the Throat Chakra – based in the middle of the throat. Colour: blue / Element: ether (space)

This chakra represents the centre of communication and our immune system is also connected though this centre. Notice as you focus on this calming blue colour flowing through the neck and the throat whether you are aware of any tightness. It's helpful to notice if you are holding onto something that has gone unsaid. If so, you can say whatever you didn't get to say to that person in your mind now and let it go, rebalancing this chakra. This area is very much an area from where we tune into speaking our truth. So it's helpful to check in with yourself and ask, "What am I communicating through here?", "What am I not communicating here?" This chakra is also about finding balance between speaking and listening and resting and doing so you don't run yourself and your immune system down. Listening to the guidance is key here. Repeat the words, "I communicate with clarity and I speak my truth", three times slowly

Bring your focus to the 6th Chakra – the Third Eye Chakra – based between the eyebrows. Colour: indigo / Element: all elements combined and light

This chakra represents your intuition and is also referred to as the eye of the soul. As you tune into the indigo colour, notice if there are feelings of being overwhelmed, confused, stressed and anxious. As you keep focusing on that area between the eyebrows, opening the eye of the soul and tuning into your intuition, let it show you what guidance is here for you, allowing you to see with more clarity and focus, calming the mind in the process and letting the thoughts settle. Imagine you have laser vision seeing straight through the confusion and everything is as clear as looking through a piece of pure ice. Surrender to the guidance of your intuition. Repeat the words, "I see the guidance clearly", three times slowly.

Bring your focus to the 7th Chakra – the Crown Chakra – based at the top of your head. Colour: purple / Element: no element or thought

This chakra represents your higher self, whatever that means to you, that feeling when you connect to the oneness and unity in the world or spiritual connection. Here you tap into the sense of being guided and knowing, exploring the sentence "I have all that I need right here within me." Sometimes when you are busy working everything out in your mind, especially speculating about how things will work out in the future, it's helpful to return to the present moment and allow yourself to focus only on the guidance here and the one thing you can do now. Bringing it back to now allows you to let go of anxiety about the situation or relationship so that you stop putting your mind into a spin about what may or may not happen in the future. As you start to trust and believe that you are guided and that everything is playing out just the way it's meant to for you, you will notice your thoughts settling. Repeat the words, "I am guided", three times slowly

To complete the Chakra Balancing exercise, start to imagine all of the chakras aligned and spinning in the same direction at the same speed. Imagine your breath and energy flowing through the body with ease. To conclude the meditation, imagine a big bright light shining from above your head and down through your body, letting the light flow down through each chakra, sealing them and keeping these aligned and cleansed energy fields protected.

May this wonderful chakra practice become a steady tool in your toolbox and one you return to again and again like a trusted friend.

"We don't see things as they are, we see them as we are."
Anais Nin

REJECTION

There are certain times in our lives when self-care becomes even more important and one of those is when we've been rejected. We definitely need self-care to regain our strength and positivity. Rejection is something most of us experience early on in our lives – it might be wanting to be friends with someone at school who doesn't feel the same. We're left hurt and wondering if it is because we are not good enough or pretty enough. The feeling of rejection never goes away, whatever age. When I first read the words, "You were not rejected you were protected", probably inspired by the words "Rejection is God's protection", it summed up in one sentence what

I had taught my clients for years – that when something doesn't work out, open yourself up to the possibility that something even more suitable and better for you will arrive instead, and that it will all make sense one day. In the moment of rejection it's hard to think that you were literally protected in that moment but, wow, when you truly choose to believe that, your mind switches immediately from a place of "poor me" to "yay me, something better is on its way".

It may take a few meditations and conversations with your friends or coach to come to that conclusion, but I can tell you it is definitely a much more compassionate way to look at it. If you are feeling rejected, repeat this affirmation, "I am protected, I am guided and I am loved", a few times. It will help you to refocus on your healing rather than on the person who has rejected you.

Looking at rejection from the other side: let's say you are letting go of someone who you have been trying to fix or save. Remember when we save others we actually prevent them from learning valuable lessons they need to evolve on their path.

"When we truly care for ourselves, it becomes possible to care far more profoundly about other people. The more alert and sensitive we are to our own needs, the more loving and generous we can be toward others."

Eda Leshan

DAY 6:
ULTIMATE SELF-CARE

We are almost at the end of the 7-day self-care plan.
I hope you are starting to enjoy taking this time for
yourself and feeling the benefits of doing the exercises,
valuing taking care of yourself and letting it become a
steady practice in your life. When I work with clients
who are feeling unloved, hopeless or lonely, they know
they need to take care of themselves, but they don't
know how to get started. The feelings that have made
them feel low may have been triggered by a relationship
difficulty, but as we have explored in the previous
chapters, it is often an old pattern that has popped up
from the past, a part of them, their inner child, that needs
some love and care. By doing this self-care visualization
you will learn how to be there for yourself at any time in
your life.

Let's visualize…

- Go ahead and close your eyes.
- Bring to mind how you are feeling in this moment.
- Try to remember a time as a child, or another time
  in your life, that you felt this way too, or if nothing
  comes to mind work with the situation present now.
- That's the part of you that is longing for love and
  support. I want you to imagine you as you are
  now going to comfort that part of yourself and
  give that part of yourself what you need. Ask
  yourself what do I need? Then tell this version of

yourself you are here to help and provide what you need and that you are enough, you are safe, heard, loved, supported, whichever words come to mind for you that feel right and comforting to you. Feel how healing this moment is as you tell yourself "You are safe with me."

Doing this is such a healing experience and it can give you a real sense of having come home within. You can talk to your younger self and tell yourself you will grow up to become confident and awesome. And when you feel at peace and you are ready, you can go ahead and open your eyes. This exercise can take as little or as long as it needs for you to feel the healing and make the peace you need to make. (Go to www.zenme.tv/mindtools for the audio version of this visualization.)

INTENTION BEHIND THE INTENTION

Have you ever found yourself saying things like, "I should really catch up with xyz so they don't get annoyed" or "I have to go to a friend's dinner tonight"? Consider the words "I should" and "I have to" – the intention behind those words is very different from "I want to". The intention is a need to please or not rock the boat – you are doing it for the other person, not for yourself. Saying no to a friend or leaving a friendship group brings the same feelings as leaving a love relationship, where you want to move on but are worried about hurting the other person.

Hanging out with the right friends can be such an uplifting experience and a real act of self-care – you can leave a conversation with a good friend feeling so elated, heard and free, but when you start filling your schedule with things you "should" do or "have to" do it will drag you down and steal your energy, leaving you exhausted. Would you want your friends to hang out with you because they feel they have to or because they truly want to? To attract that into your life you have to walk the walk yourself by making choices that are in alignment with your wishes and true intentions in relationships.

To get to the bottom of your intentions in a relationship, ask yourself: What's my intention behind hanging out with this person? And then check in and ask what's the intention behind the intention. For example, you might choose to hang out with a friend because you don't really want to be sat at home alone or because you quite fancy watching the same movie rather than because you actually want to hang out with them specifically. Then when you actually meet up you find being with them draining and realize that a night in alone, or seeing the movie alone or at a later date, would have nurtured your soul more. The clearer you become about your intentions being aligned with what you truly want in any relationship, the more you will start to attract more harmonious relationships.

The same goes for business, too: if you are going to work events because you need to and not because you want to, consider a different way of networking, perhaps online instead. The key is to choose the way you want to network – the way that's right for you, that allows your energy to flow – because if you're in a space of "I have to" it will create a heavy, blocking energy instead.

DAY 7:
NURTURED FROM INSIDE OUT

The final exercise is one I suggest to many of my clients and, although it's a pretty straightforward one, it has a multitude of benefits. I'm so grateful I came across it as it is self-care on a deeper level – an exercise that can really nurture you from the inside out.

We are going to work with the vagus nerve, which is the longest nerve running through the body from your head down through the heart and into the stomach. The vagus nerve plays a vital part as it represents the parasympathetic nervous system, which controls your heart rate, mood and digestion amongst many other important bodily functions. When you stimulate your vagus nerve through breathing, you can help lower inflammation in the body and reduce stress and anxiety. And, guess what, as well as breathing, singing at the top of your lungs is another brilliant exercise you can do to stimulate and keep the vagus nerve working for you. So next time you are singing in the shower or in your car (or is that just me?!), know that you are exercising your vagus nerve and that it has benefits way beyond lifting your mood in that moment. Yoga and laughter are also great ways to stimulate this nerve.

You can do this exercise standing or sitting with your back straight.

1. Take a deep breath in through your nose for 4 counts.
2. Exhale through the mouth for 6 counts as you purse your lips together and the air makes the sound similar to the ocean, making it audible.
3. Let the belly expand with the in-breath and drop with the out-breath.

Repeat this exercise for 3 minutes.

The goal is to slow down the breath so there are fewer breaths per minute as you breathe deeper here and allow the out-breath to be 2 counts longer than the in-breath.

YOU DID IT!

You committed and you get to reap the benefits! You can carry on using the 7-day plan or choose to use one or more of the exercises from this chapter daily, or create your own plan made up of your favourite exercises from the book. See page 168 for a checklist.

One thing I have come to believe is that creating positive habits and having a routine works! I see it time and time again with my clients, when they make space for self-care in their schedules, whether that's taking time to cook healthy meals, exercise and or meditate, their days flow with more ease, they feel less stressed and overwhelmed and, more importantly, they deal with challenges in their life more comfortably. And with everyone being "plugged in" most of the day and feeling under pressure, creating balance in our lives may mean scheduling small pockets of self-care over the day or week rather than being able to switch off each night at 6pm like in generations before us. I know that's wishful thinking to many now and that's why I help my clients schedule in self-care rituals at different times during their week to give them moments to breathe.

I hope that doing these exercises throughout the week has encouraged you to set aside at least a little time for yourself daily. Once you start making a self-care practice part of your day it soon becomes a positive habit you will never want to be without and one you can rely on to support you every day.

Mindfulness every day is an act of self-care

If you have been reading the exercises in the 7-day plan and thinking, "I wish I had more time for self-care but I don't", then I would like to remind you that you can easily introduce mindful moments into your day. You can reap the rewards by simply becoming more mindful through your daily actions: when you are sitting on a bus or train, having a cuppa, eating your lunch – these can all be mindful moments. Give yourself that time to allow for you to be doing just that one thing and for thoughts to flow in and out of your mind without needing to do anything more than acknowledge them – there is no need to judge or work anything out. Each time you notice a thought, just come back and refocus on the task at hand. One of the most beautiful things about practising mindfulness is that it allows you to just be with whatever you are feeling – accepting, for example, that you are just going to sit or be with anger allows it to actually pass through you more quickly.

I remember one morning a lady rushed into my meditation class looking all stressed out. Afterwards she told me that she almost didn't make the class because her child had taken his time as they were walking to school, pointing out a beautiful tree and some stunning flowers that he wanted to further investigate, and even stopping to say hello to someone he thought was nice. I said to her, "You rushed to get here to sit and meditate and yet you missed all the signs your son gave you of practising mindfulness on the way to school." She looked at me completely confused and then the penny dropped, "Wow my son was fully present and in my mind I was already in the car driving to the studio!" Don't let the special moments of the present get away, those are magical and deeply bonding in any relationship. So before we go blaming anyone else for their behaviour, it's good to tune in and ask "Am I fully present in this relationship?" So much can be solved when we hold space for each other and truly see, feel and hear each other.

Go forward with self-love

Throughout the book, as you have worked your way
through becoming more self-aware and accepting, learnt
how to love yourself and take care of yourself, you will have
peeled back those layers to find the issues lying at the core
of whichever relationship you were working on when you
started this journey. You have allowed yourself to perceive
the relationship and yourself in different ways, learnt from
it and taken the opportunity to heal what was unhealed
within you.

I truly hope that the book and the exercises have inspired
you to know that whatever challenging relationships you
are faced with, you have the tools to return to for support
whenever needed. Hopefully you will approach relationship
issues with a newfound curiosity and allow yourself to
figure out what that challenge is there to teach you. I also
hope that it has reminded you of how powerful you are
when you take back your control and focus on you.

You can now go forward with a deeper understanding
of yourself and an abundance of compassion and self-love,
yes? If not, I suggest returning to the self-love chapter
and repeating the exercises, until you can shout YES to
that question!!! Remember, I told you, you deserve to
LOVE yourself!

Celebrating You

Thank you for going on this journey with me through the book. It's been an honour to support you. I hope by now you know that you are an amazing human being put on this earth for a reason. Never let anyone convince you that you have to dim your beautiful light so that they don't feel inferior. The world needs you and your light, so shine it as brightly as you can – there is room for everyone. And if you ever have a moment of doubt, a little stumble, know that you are not alone – we all have those moments. Say these words to pick yourself back up. From my heart to yours

I am love
I am a beautiful radiant light
I am safe
I am enough
I am
And so it is

Love & Light
Camilla x

I hope to connect with you either online @camilladallerup or in person at one of my workshops or classes.

CHECKLIST OF EXERCISES

1. SELF-AWARENESS

☐ Relationship inventory
☐ Thought mapping
☐ Relationship check-in
☐ What negative stories have you created?
☐ Hello beautiful!
☐ What are you projecting?
☐ Illusion or truth?
☐ Tackling your resistance
☐ Staying true to yourself
☐ Become a master at manifesting
☐ Raw-form journalling – download your thoughts

2. SELF-ACCEPTANCE

☐ Me right here, right now
☐ Mindfulness exercise
☐ Filling the void
☐ Grieving an unrealized dream
☐ U-turn your thoughts with gratitude
☐ Accept and switch it
☐ Letting go meditation
☐ Cutting the cord visualization
☐ I forgive myself as I forgive you
☐ Let's celebrate you
☐ Mirror exercise

3. SELF-LOVE
- ☐ What do you believe about yourself?
- ☐ Are you enough?
- ☐ Be your own best friend
- ☐ Ignite the love
- ☐ Reframe – what is and isn't true about what you think of yourself?
- ☐ Working out your needs
- ☐ A love letter to yourself
- ☐ In the mirror
- ☐ Self-compassion and you
- ☐ Create a self-love ritual
- ☐ Hypnotic visualization – falling in love with myself

4. SELF-CARE
- ☐ Day 1: Morning ritual
- ☐ Day 2: Fuel your joy
- ☐ Day 3: Let the love flow
- ☐ Day 4: Divorce your bad habits
- ☐ Day 5: Chakra balancing
- ☐ Day 6: Ultimate self-care
- ☐ Day 7: Nurtured from inside out

RESOURCES

Articles

Epigentics: www.brucelipton.com/resource/article/epigenetics

'Bad is Stronger than Good': http://assets.csom.umn.edu/assets/71516.pdf

'When Good is Stronger than Bad': http://www.rickhanson.net/teaching/tgc-public-summary/

'Greater Self-Acceptance Improves Emotional Wellbeing: https://www.health.harvard.edu/blog/greater-self-acceptance-improves-emotional-well-201605169546

'How the Universe Views Intimate Relationships': https://www.elevatedexistence.com/marianne-williamson-how-the-universe-views-intimate-relationships

'The Scary Power of Negative Words': https://goop.com/wellness/mindfulness/the-scary-power-of-negative-words

'Can Plants Really Get Upset?": https://www.dailymail.co.uk/femail/article-5703247/Bizarre-experiment-shows-talking-plants-thrive.html

'IKEA conducts bullying experiment on plants – the results are shocking': https://globalnews.ca/news/4217594/bully-a-plant-ikea/

Marianne Williamson: https://marianne.com

'Living Beyond Limits': Amy Purdy: https://www.ted.com/talks/amy_purdy_living_beyond_limits?language=en

'When two TV greats meet: Oprah opens up on her traumatic childhood during David Letterman lecture series: https://www.dailymail.co.uk/tvshowbiz/

article-2239102/Oprah-Winfrey-opens-traumatic-childhood-David-Letterman-lecture-series.html
'Scientific Proof that Negative Beliefs Harm Your Health':
Dr. Lissa Rankin: https://www.mindbodygreen.com/0-9690/scientific-proof-that-negative-beliefs-harm-your-health.html
'Mindfulness of Feeling Tones': http://summitmindfulness.com/2016/09/mindfulness-of-feeling-tones/
'Love Yourself to Stay Healthy': https://www.newscientist.com/article/dn19575-love-yourself-to-stay-healthy/
'Self-esteem and autonomic physiology: Self-esteem levels predict cardiac vagal tone': https://www.sciencedirect.com/science/article/abs/pii/S0092656610000929?via%3Dihub
https://www.rcpsych.ac.uk/pdf/Heart,%20Mind%20and%20Spirit%20%20Mohamed%20Salem.pdf
'5 tips to stop negative self-talk once and for all': https://www.jackcanfield.com/blog/negative-self-talk/

Books

Anderson, Simone, *Journey to Health* (Allen & Unwin)
Berman, Ph.D, Laura, *Quantum Love* (Hay House)
Brach, Tara, Ph.D., *Radical Acceptance* (Bantam)
Cameron, Julie, *The Artist's Way* (TarcherPerigee)
Chopra M.D., Deepak and Tanzi Ph.D., Rudolph E., *The Healing Self* (Harmony)
Chopra, Deepak, *The Seven Spiritual Laws of Success* (New World Library)
Davidji, *Secrets of Meditation* (Hay House)
Desmond, Tim, *The Self-Compassion Skills Workbook* (W.W. Norton & Co)

Dyer, Dr. Wayne W., *The Power of Intention* (Hay House)

Foundation for Inner Peace, *A Course in Miracles*
(Foundation for Inner Peace)

Hagen, Steve, *Buddhism Plain and Simple* (Broadway
Books)

Hamilton, David R., *I Heart Me: The Science of Self-Love*
(Hay House)

Hanson, Rick, *Buddha's Brain* (New Harbinger
Publications)

Hawkins, M.D, Ph.D, David R., *Letting Go, The Pathway of
Surrender* (Hay House)

Hicks, Esther, Hicks, Jerry, *The Vortex* (Hay House)

Kabat-Zinn, Jon, *Meditation Is Not What You Think*
(Hachette Books)

Mason, Keith, *Thoughts That Harm, Thoughts That Heal*
(Piatkus Books)

Michels, Barry, Stutz, Phil, *The Tools* (Spiegel & Grau)

Peer, Marisa, *I Am Enough* (One Edition)

Pfender, April, *Chakra Balance* (Althea Press)

Rippentrop, Ph.D., Betsy, Adamson, Eve, *The Complete
Idiot's Guide to Chakra* (Alpha)

Ruiz, Don Miguel, *The Four Agreements* (Amber-Allen
Publishing)

Saradananda, Swami, *The Essential Guide to Chakras*
(Watkins)

Tolle, Eckhart, *The Power of Now* (Namaste Publishing)

ACKNOWLEDGEMENTS

When we are being challenged by a relationship, we don't think "one day I'll be grateful for this and for the hurt and frustration", but with time we realize that every challenge is an opportunity to grow within. I have learnt so much about myself through relationships, some that I continue to learn from and some that only came into my life to wake me up to the wounds that I needed to heal. I'm grateful for them all. The most painful were those that cracked me open the most and pushed me to make some seriously important decisions for myself! I am forever a teacher and a student, and I want to thank all of my clients. The way they have invited me into their lives and their challenges has inspired me and wanted me to always learn more, study and evolve both as a coach and as an individual. They have taught me as much as I have taught them and for that I am thankful.

I was raised by two extremely good humans – my mum, who taught me never to give up if you believe in something, and my dad, who has a level of patience that's beyond belief. He taught me that sometimes it's okay to slow down and go at your own pace. Their support can be felt always, even though we live thousands of miles apart – I love you mum and dad! And thank you to my sister, who is a rock to me always. If I am ever overwhelmed, I know who to call. I'm so lucky to have a best friend as a sister.

Thank you to my meditation community at Unplug Meditation in LA. I love you all. I feel extremely grateful that we have such a special place to connect and support each other, and that I have meditation, dear friends and colleagues to turn to when I'm having an off day.

And thank you to author Yung Pueblo, whose work I admire so much. Thank you for writing the foreword to this book – you are such an inspiration and I'm grateful for the way you share your work with the world and inspire people like me. Thank you so much and keep shining your light brightly!

Thank you to my wonderful editor, Dawn Bates. I said it in the last book and I'm going to say it again – I can't imagine how I would have done it without you. Thank you for brainstorming with me and helping me stick to deadlines, and for your expertise and your guidance. I believe you are an angel sent to help me through the book-writing journey. So much love and gratitude for you landing in my life.

And to my publisher, Jo Lal – wow, I can't believe here we are with book number three. It seems only like yesterday we had our very first meeting and you took a bet on me with book number one. Although sometimes I need a few days to digest your feedback, mainly because it is honest and constructive and it pushes me right outside my comfort zone, I know 100 per cent you always have my best interests at heart and it always helps me push me further than I would have ever pushed myself. All of your support, and that of everyone at Watkins, means the world to me – thank you. I'm so very proud to be a Watkins' author, a company with such integrity.

And Kevin, my husband, thank you for always being so understanding and supportive and I'm sorry you didn't see me much last year whilst I was writing. Thank you for cooking me delicious meals and giving me the love and space to create this book. I love you!

Sven, our beloved dog, I dedicate this book to you. You taught me more about relationships than I could have ever imagined. Your calming energy and unconditional love was so special – the late-night cuddles and meditations when I was writing but tired, and wondering what the next words would be, energized and inspired me. I still can't believe we had to say goodbye to you. The grieving is real, but so are all of the magical memories of you. You will live on in our hearts whilst you will no doubt be chasing baseballs in heaven. Thank you for the 10 years you chose to be with us and for showing me how loving with an open heart looks and feels.

WATKINS
Sharing Wisdom Since 1893

The story of Watkins began in 1893, when scholar of esotericism John Watkins founded our bookshop, inspired by the lament of his friend and teacher Madame Blavatsky that there was nowhere in London to buy books on mysticism, occultism or metaphysics. That moment marked the birth of Watkins, soon to become the publisher of many of the leading lights of spiritual literature, including Carl Jung, Rudolf Steiner, Alice Bailey and Chögyam Trungpa.

Today, the passion at Watkins Publishing for vigorous questioning is still resolute. Our stimulating and groundbreaking list ranges from ancient traditions and complementary medicine to the latest ideas about personal development, holistic wellbeing and consciousness exploration. We remain at the cutting edge, committed to publishing books that change lives.

DISCOVER MORE AT:
www.watkinspublishing.com

Read our blog

Watch and listen to
our authors in action

Sign up to
our mailing list

We celebrate conscious, passionate, wise and happy living.
Be part of that community by visiting

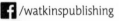 /watkinspublishing   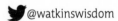 @watkinswisdom

 /watkinsbooks    @watkinswisdom